PUEBLO DECO

PUEBLO DECO

Photographs and text by Carla Breeze

RIZZOLI
NEW YORK

For Merlebird, my Theo

FRONTISPIECE
The S.H. Kress Department Store in El Paso, Texas.

FRONT COVER
Detail of the KiMo Theater in Albuquerque, New Mexico.

BACK COVER
LEFT, Detail of terra-cotta chevrons from the Gramercy House apartments, New York.

TOP RIGHT
Detail of the United States Post Office in Gallup, New Mexico.

MIDDLE RIGHT
Detail of the Federal Building in Albuquerque, New Mexico.

BOTTOM RIGHT
The S.H. Kress Department Store in El Paso, Texas.

First published in the United States of America in 1990 by
RIZZOLI INTERNATIONAL PUBLICATIONS, INC.
300 Park Avenue South, New York, NY 10010

Library of Congress Cataloging-in-Publication Data

Breeze, Carla.
   Pueblo deco / photographs and text by Carla Breeze.
      p.   cm.
   Includes bibliographical references.
   ISBN 0-8478-1177-8 (pbk.)
   1. Art deco (Architecture)—United States.
2. Architecture, Modern-20th century—United States.   3. Pueblos—Southwest, New—Influence.   I. Title.
[NA712.5.A7B7   1990]
720′.973′09041—dc20   89-43570
                                                              CIP

Designed by Charles Davey
Set in type by Rainsford Type, Danbury, Connecticut
Printed and bound in Singapore

CONTENTS

Polychrome terra-cotta graces the exterior of the Gramercy House apartments of 1928 in New York City.

PREFACE

You get into your car and drive. It's faster than traveling by horse, and you pass through oceans of sagebrush, see the Sangre de Cristo mountains in the distance. When you get to Raton (Spanish for "rat"), you find a courthouse. Standing in front of the Colfax County Courthouse, in contemplation before making any photographs, you realize that its architects must have loved this region, the cowboys who settled here, and the Pueblo Indians. Rising in stepped setbacks, the building has a red-tiled roof, revealing the influence of Spanish architecture. Above the doors are cast-zinc panels with the brands ranchers used to identify their cattle. Each detail is lovingly designed and is an homage to the indigenous: Art Deco, yet distinctively Southwestern.

It was the KiMo Theater that started me on the quest to find and photograph examples of the Pueblo Deco style. As a child I had been overwhelmed more by the theater itself than by any movies screened there. Built in 1927 in Albuquerque, the KiMo fulfills its Indian name, "King of its Kind." The façade is dripping with terra-cotta Hopi sun shields and tile kachina masks. The interior is equally colorful. Murals, wrought-iron water birds, and a ceiling painted with stylized animals are illuminated by an unearthly glow emanating from light fixtures shaped from terra-cotta to resemble cow skulls.

This book would not have been possible without the following people: other researchers who have preceded me, preservationists, architectural historians, and the numerous others who care about buildings.

Marcus Whiffen's past collaboration with me and his staunch support of my work have been invaluable. Individuals of his stature often don't have the interest or time to devote to another person's work as unstintingly as he has. Wayne Decker's contributions have made it possible for me to translate what I see onto film. Without the assistance of Ernst Wildi (technical director at Hasselblad), many of the photographs of details would not have been feasible. Bernice Thomas, a scholar working on a monograph of Edward F. Sibbert's work (funded by the S. H. Kress

Foundation), has been a wonderful resource, sharing her knowledge and sources with me with an openness that is rare.

Other people gave me access to specific buildings, and without them the interior photographs could not have been made: Ed Hardy and John Poimiroo at the Ahwahnee Hotel; Beverly Thomas at the Texas & Pacific Passenger Terminal; D. Ryan Smith, the director of the Panhandle Plains Museum; Mr. and Mrs. Herman Riley, owners of the Pueblo Cafe in the Shaffer Hotel; Gordon Church at the KiMo Theater; Dr. and Mrs. James Hopkins, owners of the McArthur House; Jerry Massee, president of La Fonda Hotel; Pat Eatherly of the Will Rogers Memorial Center; Mike Dibb, manager of the Plaza Hotel in El Paso; Beau Sangre at the Indian Hospital; Ed Allcorn of the Paramount Theater; Ray Deduicon, conductor at Southern Pacific; and Skip Maisel at Maisel's Trading Post.

My family gave up our horses by the time I was grown, so for other modes of transportation

I'm indebted to Merle O'Keeffe, Trish and Bruce Moxon, Bill J. Shelton, Alan Isaacson, and that sweetheart of the desert, Cindi Doisy, who was my roping partner for some of this.

David Gebhard's constructive review affected the reconsideration of Frank Lloyd Wright's work in the Southwest. Carol Naille at Amfac in Flagstaff was enormously helpful with the Mary E. J. Colter drawings in their Fred Harvey Collection and other related materials. Dr. Mary Ann Anders and her staff at the New Mexico Historic Preservation Division have done excellent research for the various cultural and preservation nominations their office prepares. She was especially accessible and made every effort to provide me with copies of their research. Claire Kuehn at the Panhandle Plains Museum provided me with documents from their archives she thought might be useful. Herbert Mitchell of Avery Library was instrumental in steering me around both their collections and those at the New York Public Library.

Virginia Gratton's research for her monograph on Colter's work was extremely useful. Gratton's point that a major element of Colter's aesthetics was a worn, used look was especially influential on my photographs. Often, buildings were not in the best state of repair, and I've tried to work with this factor rather than eliminate any images which might indicate the processes of time and use.

I am also indebted to: Pavel Opocensky, Susan Mayr, Fundamental Photo, Rod Replogle, Marv Steputis, Ossie and Julius Decker, Joyce Gibson, Bill O'Keeffe, Joe E. Seward, Mary L. Shelton, and Kenneth Lee—all gave me assistance at various times during this project; J. Gaut's drawing of the S. H. Kress building in Amarillo was an unsolicited surprise; and Jackie Sarfati's typing and translation of my handwriting was appreciated. The conversations I have had over the years with Marcelina Calabaza and Edwina Garcia have been illuminating. I feel fortunate that our friendship has crossed the cultural rivers. May this book contribute to the survival of the Pueblos and all other Indian Nations and our appreciation of the Southwest.

INTRODUCTION

The Wild West has rustled the imagination of the American public since nineteenth-century U. S. government expeditions explored the region. As train tracks raced across the continent, travelers sought to experience the sublime and awesome landscape, the immense Grand Canyon, rugged mountain ranges, and mauve deserts under a cobalt sky. The intense sunlight had an elemental quality. By the turn of the century, the man who would eventually market the Southwest for consumption was providing hotels for travelers along the Atchison and Topeka Railroad lines. Fred Harvey, restaurateur and hotelier, knew what these "tenderfeet" from the East wanted: adventure *and* running water. Travelers wanted the scent of Indian fry bread wafting on desert air without risk of dying from thirst. They wanted to tramp about seemingly transient towns built of mud without fear of rattlesnakes. And often these same travelers simply wanted to immerse themselves in the ambience of the area without leaving the train station.

Catering to this desire, the Fred Harvey Company and designer Mary Colter worked on the first experiment in packaging the Indian and Spanish cultures of the Southwest, the Alvarado Hotel. Built at Albuquerque's train station in 1902, this was a bold move to imitate traditional Spanish mission architecture. Regardless of the exterior, it was the Indian Room at the hotel that was most popular. Designed as the interior of a Pueblo abode, the room's walls were covered with Navajo Eyedazzler rugs (so named for their brilliant colors). Zuni and Acoma pottery was everywhere. The room was filled with Hopi kachinas, Apache baskets from the White Mountains, silver and turquoise jewelry, steer horns,

and any other saleable curios that might appeal to tourists.

The Indian Room mitigated the need to venture into Indian Pueblos or leave the comfort of the hotel to encounter the exotic. Women from Isleta Pueblo in print dresses and fringed shawls, with wares they had made, stood under the hotel's arcade. In the verdant patio a fountain splashed, reminiscent of Mexico. For the more venturesome, Harvey provided tours led by young women educated in the history and lore of the region. These guides would take the tourists, packed into touring cars, into mountain valleys to visit small Hispanic churches. Or they would drive to San Felipe Pueblo, sited on a black mesa of volcanic lava, where Corn Dancers might be performing sacred rituals to invoke rain.

So successful was the experiment that Fred Harvey (as the company was referred to even after its founder's death) embarked on an extensive building campaign, often in conjunction with the Atchison Topeka & Santa Fe Railroad, creating the magnificent Union station in Los Angeles, El Tovar at the Grand Canyon, and El Navajo Hotel in Gallup, New Mexico.

El Navajo synthesized everything Colter

learned from designing the Indian Room at the Alvarado. El Navajo didn't have an Indian Room, it *was* Indian. Every detail, from door handles to chandeliers, used motifs and designs from Navajo sand paintings, such as Yeh figures which are stylized humans. Indeed, sand paintings so inspired the decor that Colter found a means of affixing them to panels and hung them about the lobby instead of paintings. The 1923 opening of the hotel was attended by senators and socialites; medicine men provided the blessing ceremony. Creating a sensation, the event was reported in sources as far away as the *Washington Post.* Colter had created an appetite for anything and everything Indian.

When returning home, tourists stuffed pottery, blankets, and jewelry into their valises as mementos of their trip. Designers in the Southwest, and eventually in other regions, were influenced by the arts and architecture so flamboyantly marketed by Fred Harvey.

Simultaneously, the Art Deco movement was gaining momentum and international recognition as a result of the 1925 Paris Exposition. Deco's emphasis on ethnic and geometric ornament coincided with Colter's style, Pueblo Deco. She had seen how the cubistic forms of Pueblo and Spanish architecture could be juxtaposed with geometric decoration inspired by Pueblo and other Native American motifs.

Another designer, Inez B. Westlake, produced highly distinctive work, similarly derived by integrating regionalism with contemporary aesthetics. Westlake worked with Trost and Trost, whose designs for the Hotel Franciscan were widely published. The Boller Brothers from St. Louis were designing theaters all over the Midwest, and they hired Westlake to contribute her

talents to a theater inspired by the Pueblo and Navajo Indians, the KiMo in Albuquerque. It was appropriate that this fabulous theater in the Pueblo Deco style would be dedicated to the people who had originally settled the Southwest.

Arriving from another continent thousands of years before, the Indians who settled on the plateaus and valleys of the Rio Grande evolved a culture that accommodated this harsh landscape. Pyramidal structures of mud and stone rose on the mesas. Prickly-pear cactus provided its orange fruit. Baskets were woven from river grasses and reeds. Pueblo Indian ritual life revolved around the life-giving properties of rain.

The sixteenth-century Spanish invasion of the region affected the Indian's architectural traditions. Windows and doors replaced roof entries. Fireplaces replaced fire pits. Christianity mingled

ABOVE LEFT
The stucco details of the entrance to the McKinley County Courthouse in Gallup, New Mexico, are a variation of the cumulus cloud motif.

LEFT
The façade of the McKinley County Courthouse contains heavily modeled and stuccoed forms derived from adobe construction and flat-arched fenestration.

ABOVE
After the Navajos had contact with reservation traders in the late nineteenth century, figurative imagery began to supplement the standard geometric designs of their textiles, as in this Navajo weaving from the 1920s.

OPPOSITE
The eighteenth-century mission church of Pecos Pueblo, in eastern New Mexico, was inspirational to twentieth-century architects.

9

with kiva rituals, and mission churches were built at the Pueblos. After realizing that the Seven Cities of Cibola they were in search of were mythical, the *conquistadores* settled down to wrest a living by farming and by trading. A route led from Santa Fe through Chihuahua to Mexico City, following the trade route used by the prehistoric Indians to obtain copper bells and macaw feathers from the Aztecs.

The Athabascan Indians, nomadic Apaches and Navajos, arrived at the time of the Hispanic influx. Stealing the horses introduced to the area by the Spanish, these tribes preyed on sedentary Pueblo and Hispanic peoples. The Pueblo, Hispanic, and Athabascan cultures never entirely merged, but borrowed from each other to create a viable way of life.

Some architects came to the Southwest for their health. The aridity was believed to cure tuberculosis. Once there, they were charmed by the adobe architecture and Indian arts. John Gaw Meem applied Hopi rain clouds to an administration building on the University of New Mexico campus. Henry C. Trost, who had worked in Chicago, moved west and applied heads of Spanish *conquistadores* to a Deco skyscraper in Phoenix. An anonymous architect used Zuni turquoise jewelry as inspiration for a trading-post façade in Albuquerque. The Hopi sun motif appeared in a wrought-iron grille at a bank in Denver. At Bisbee, Arizona, a miner crouches while panning for gold on a frieze over the entrance of the courthouse. Cowboys ride across the façade of a courthouse in New Mexico. Pueblo Deco even made scattered forays into New York City. English architect Alfred Bossom, for example, decorated his apartment in New York City with Indian motifs.

Always appreciative of the vernacular, Frank Lloyd Wright utilized the stepped pyramid in his work after visiting the Southwest and seeing Hopi Pueblo. Literal references to the Indian appeared in the sculptures he designed to flank a country-club entrance in Wisconsin—a chief and his squaw.

The Great Crash of 1929 dampened excessive and ebullient decoration using terra-cotta,

The McArthur House in the Country Club district of Phoenix is a sophisticated integration of traditional elements, such as a campanile, and modernist masses and forms.

The Big Chief Theater in Gallup, New Mexico, was converted into commercial space when television eroded movie theater profits.

INSET
Set on a hill, the tiered and oval-shaped Tovrea Castle in Phoenix was built in 1926 by an Italian immigrant, Allesio Carraro, and his son.

expensive marbles, and brass in many parts of the country. Sustained by the gas and oil boom in the West, however, new construction was not as constrained there and Pueblo Deco was still the rage. Fred Harvey even decorated train cars in this style.

Harvey's only problem was that he decided he knew the Indian culture better than the Indians. The company mandated that jewelry produced by Indian artisans for his company incorporate bows and arrows and other kitsch motifs. During the late thirties the Pueblo Deco style degenerated. The ultimate blow to Pueblo Deco, aside from the depression and World War II, was the advent of the automobile and the airplane. Few people now traveled by train, and Harvey's marketing techniques were borrowed and used to create roadside architecture, concrete tepees, and log cabins.

Fred Harvey made a vague attempt to transfer the Pueblo Deco style to airports. Spanish *señoritas*, "Harvey Girls," served margaritas and Mexican food to travelers in the subdued puebloid Albuquerque Airport, but the original elegance and richness of Harvey Houses such as El Navajo could not be replicated after the thirties.

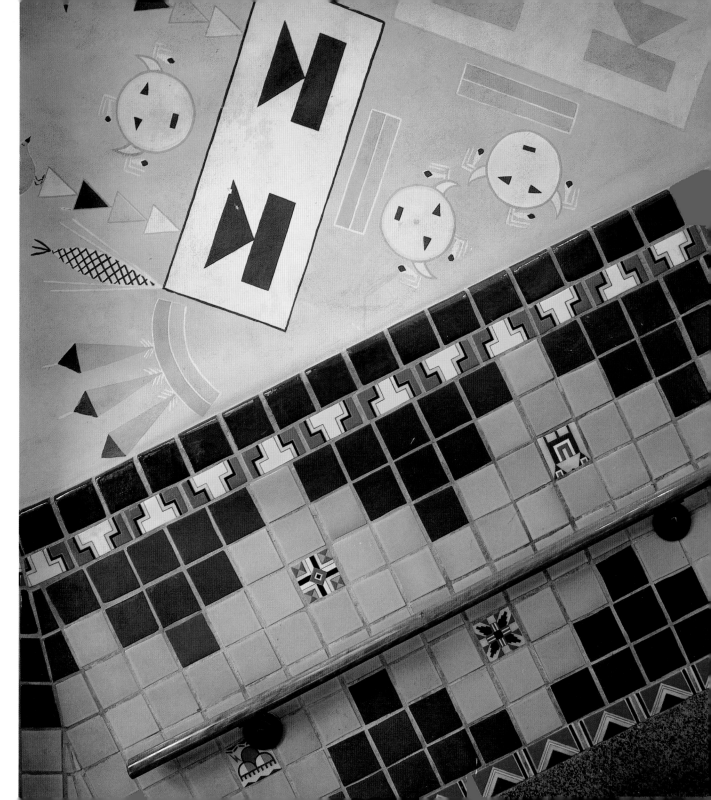

OPPOSITE FAR LEFT
The seventeenth-century church at Quarai, New Mexico, one of the few masonry churches built by the Pueblo, was abandoned because of Comanche and Apache raids.

OPPOSITE LEFT
Navajo directional motifs alternate with circles in a band below the parapet of the Swastika Hotel in Raton, New Mexico. Built in 1915, the hotel is typical of brick vernacular architecture in the West.

RIGHT
Terra-cotta tile wainscoting in the lobby of the McKinley County Courthouse in Gallup, New Mexico, enhances the WPA murals of Lloyd Moylan, whose Indian motifs were inspired by Kiva painting.

ONE

TRAIN STATIONS AND DETOURS

"What do we want with this vast waterless area—this region of savages and wild beasts, of deserts, of drifting sands and whirlwinds and dust, of cactus and prairie dogs? To what use could we ever hope to put these great deserts...?"(1) How alien and daunting the Southwest seemed to Daniel Webster when he wrote this in 1854.

It is a region that now encompasses western Texas, southern Colorado, New Mexico, Arizona, and southern Utah and California. The few rivers transforming narrow valleys into lush oases ebb and flow depending on rain and snowfall. A roaring muddy assault in the spring, the Rio Grande is a mere trickle among mud flats by July. During sporadic rains, water dashes against hardened earth, parched from months of drought, creating *arroyos*, or temporary stream beds.

By the time the Spanish settlers made a formal *entrada*, a colonial effort sanctioned by the Spanish crown, they too must have wondered about the value of this venture into such a harsh environment. Believing myths and exaggerated accounts of a few tentative explorers, the king of Spain was excited by the possibility of still greater riches and the abundance of heathen

OPPOSITE
Even the turnbuckles of the entrance canopy at the Texas & Pacific Railroad terminal in Fort Worth have decorative casings embellished with the building's motif— the stepped pyramid.

souls to be saved. He approved the *entrada*, which thrust 2,000 miles north of Mexico City.

Even the name *California* was derived from a Spanish fictional account of paradise, *Las Sergas de Esplandian*. Explorers recounting their feats indicated that Seven Cities of Cibola (in the northern Sonora Desert now encompassing the Southwest) had been founded by a Christian archbishop, his six bishops, and their brethren. Having fled, as did many Christians, from the Moorish invasion blanketing Spain, they had reputedly settled among Indians who wove fine cotton textiles and lived amid wealth and luxury. Rumors reported that the Indians wore pearls and emeralds and that their dwellings glittered with gold. After the stunning wealth encountered by the Spanish among the Aztec and Mayan nations, these reports and rumors didn't seem improbable.

Francisco Vasquez de Coronado led the colonizers through jungles, over treacherous mountains, and finally through the arduous Sonora Desert, only to arrive in 1541 at what is now Zuni Pueblo, an Indian village of loosely scattered mud houses. There they found neither gold nor emeralds. The Zuni Indians wove fine cotton textiles and adorned themselves for rituals with mother-of-pearl and turquoise, but the wealth imagined by the Spanish simply didn't exist.

After the Spaniards established military control of the region (of a sort—the Pueblo Indians revolted 139 years later), missions were established by the Franciscans. The Spanish government supplied the friars with "building kits," which included plans, materials, and tools, to facilitate the construction of churches and subsidiary structures. The mission at Santo Domingo Pueblo, built in the sixteenth century, still stands. The purpose of the missions, aside from the conversion of the Indians to Christianity, was to exert political control over the aboriginal population by organizing them into work forces. Initial conversion and participation were achieved through outright bribery. "Gifts" of livestock, seeds, and metal tools persuaded the Indians to construct secular and religious buildings, farm fields, and generally provide manual labor.

Eventually, the Spanish established a capital at Santa Fe, and small farming communities fanned out into the surrounding mountain valleys. Communications and trade between Santa Fe and Mexico were slow and costly. Settlers had to rely on their own skills. Barter was the primary form of business transaction in the region.

Villages were planned around plazas, similar in concept to the prehistoric Pueblo urban centers. The church was usually the most prominent building, with a cloister next to it and schoolrooms and secular buildings on its other side. Houses were built along simple grids emanating from the plaza. Most houses and secular buildings were built with adobe. A few churches were built of masonry, constructed by Indians who had already developed their own fine masonry techniques prior to the arrival of the Hispanics.

The Anasazi, Hohokam, and Mogollon Indians were gradually quelled as well as decimated by new diseases. Various pueblos managed to survive at their original locations—the Hopis on their mesas, the Zuni, and Taos for example—but the majority were destroyed or moved to different locations.

Life for the Spanish continued to be tenuous. Only infrequently was it lightened by religious and secular celebrations. The annual fair at Taos, where French fur traders appeared, was the most exciting event. A temporary peace during the fair encouraged trade between the Native Americans (even the Comanches and Apaches who were known for their ferocity) and the settlers.

The expanding American colonies began to make their presence felt by the early nineteenth century. Boundaries were pushed westward. Zebulon Pike was the earliest American explorer to reach the Southwest, and traders soon followed. Slippers, calicos, silks, dress patterns, and metal tools found their way into Hispanic and Indian households. It wasn't long before settlers from the United States wanted to move west in search of agricultural and commercial opportunities.

Mexican independence had little effect on the Southwest. The greatest impact came with the subsequent Mexican loss of the war with the United States.

The transcontinental railroad built by the Central Pacific and the Union Pacific finally gave the Southwest access to the outside world. Spurs were built by Southern Pacific and Texas & Pacific, reaching into this isolated wasteland. Native Americans recoiled from the advent of the "iron horse," realizing not only that their way of life was changed forever by colonization, but that this new form of transportation could only infringe further on their cultures. As hunters demolished buffalo herds from train windows, and reservation lines were continually redrawn or pushed back, these fears became reality.

When William H. Jackson returned with detailed photographs from a U.S. Geological Survey in 1876, Congress was astonished by the landscape found in the Southwest. Fabulous canyons flayed the earth's crust; rough mountains loomed from the plains of the Llano Estacado.

Even more incredible, Indians had lived against vast cliffs for centuries, building masonry towers and apartmentlike housing under the shelter of Mesa Verde, Montezuma Castle, and at Betakin.

The man who was the first Anglo (non-Indian or Hispanic) to raft down the Colorado River, the last unexplored region of the continental United States, was also the first director of the U.S. Bureau of American Ethnology (BAE), John Wesley Powell. Ten years after reviewing Jackson's photographs and reading Powell's accounts, Congress was sufficiently impressed with the region to fund further research through the BAE.

As director, Powell encouraged the study of Pueblo architecture. Private funding indicated greater public interest in Native American antiquities, allowing Pueblo Bonito at Chaco Canyon in the Four Corners area of New Mexico to be excavated by the Wetherill brothers, early archaeologists. Archaeological excavations were finally feasible because of the advent of the railroad. So while it eroded native culture, the railroad also made preservation of prehistoric sites possible.

The Atchison Topeka & Santa Fe Railroad (known popularly as the Santa Fe) reached Raton, New Mexico, by 1878 (at gunpoint—the frenzy for expanding railroad lines was so intense).

To promote the Santa Fe and lure tourism west, the railroad seized on the theme "See America First." Artists were commissioned to create brochures and posters depicting the magnificent landscape with its surreal pinks, ochres, mauves, and reds, and its natural wonders, inhabited by Pueblo, Navajo, and Plains Indians.

To mesh advertising and product, the management realized that hotels and restaurants would have to be built to accommodate tourism. These amenities could even be incorporated into the advertising campaigns, particularly if they mirrored the rich cultures and surrounding environment, an experience so different from that of the East Coast.

Thanks to Fred Harvey, the Santa Fe already enjoyed a distinguished reputation. Prior to the formation of his company, travelers were obliged to grab a meal wherever the train stopped. Service of a meal often coincided with the departing train whistle. Faced with this choice, the traveler usually eschewed the meal. Who wanted to be left behind on the dry dusty plains with the next station or train miles and miles away? This situation arose by design and collusion: Railroads received kickbacks for any uneaten meals. After working as an agent for various lines and experiencing the rigors of traveling without decent dining, Fred Harvey became associated with the Atchison Topeka & Santa Fe, opening his first restaurant in Topeka, Kansas.

In 1876 it was novel to serve gourmet meals to travelers. Even more astonishing, Harvey insisted on serving the finest quality food available in a pleasant and relaxing atmosphere complete with linens and exquisite place settings. Although a jacket was always required (and one provided for those without), the emphasis was on the dining experience. As the Santa Fe expanded, so did Fred Harvey. Harvey facilities were distinguished by their attention to detail, no matter how isolated the location. Boxcars in Winslow, Arizona, were painted on the exterior with large, bold motifs from Navajo blankets. The interiors reflected Harvey's usual standards.

There was one exception to the jacket regulation: Santa Fe. Adopting the casual dress of the artists and writers who were popularizing the place, the company suspended its dress code in the La Fonda Hotel. (Those cowboys in Dodge City who insisted on dining without jackets should have moved to Santa Fe.) Still, horses were never allowed indoors, regardless of the locale. At the Casteñada in Las Vegas, New Mexico, several rode in on their mounts to find Mr. Harvey confronting them. Calmly, he insisted that proper behavior be observed, if only for the sake of the ladies present.

Fred Harvey was just as concerned as the Santa Fe with marketing the natural wonders and cultures of Indian Country. Together they built stations, restaurants, and hotels around Southwestern themes. A precedent for the utilization of Spanish Colonial and Mission styles had already occurred. A. Page Brown's California Building at the 1893 Chicago World's Fair was one of the earliest buildings to revive these styles. Spanish missions in California romantically evoked both the Hispanic and the Indian cultures. Simple masses with articulated walls were broken by arcades and arched doorways. These forms could be adapted in a variety of ways. Charles F. Whittlesey was the chief architect for AT & SF, and he worked with Fred Harvey designing stations and hotels. Sadly, many of the hotels are now gone.

The architect and designer most responsible for the Fred Harvey "look" was Mary Elizabeth Jane Colter. Having studied at the California School of Design (later the San Francisco Art Institute) and then apprenticed with a local architect, Colter's first job with the Harvey Company was as a design consultant. She was hired to conceive and decorate the Indian Room and shop at the Alvarado Hotel. The idea for an Indian Room was that of Herman Schweizer, who was a buyer for the company's shops. He could see the potential in commissioning and selling Indian rugs, baskets, jewelry, and other arts. In 1901, an Indian Department became a division of the company. Shortly thereafter, Fred Harvey died. After his death, Harvey's sons continued the company's expansion and its traditions.

Colter arranged the sales and display areas more like a museum than a retail space. She combined roughhewn furniture made to specification with Hispanic antiques. Apache baskets hung from rafters. Tlingit blankets sewn with buttons hung on the walls. Navajo rugs decorated the wooden floors. Pottery from every Pueblo abounded. She even employed women from Isleta Pueblo to make pottery and Navajo women to weave for the edification of tourists. Other Indians brought their handicrafts and arts to sell on the large veranda outside the hotel. The result of her work was so successful that tourists who visited the Alvarado in Albuquerque raved to others.

When the Santa Fe purchased a line running from Williams, Arizona, to the copper mines at Anita, it became possible to supplant the day-long stagecoach ride from Flagstaff to the Grand Canyon with railway service. Mary Colter found herself employed again, working with Charles Whittlesey on accommodations and supplementary structures for tourism.

El Tovar, a hotel at the Grand Canyon designed by Colter, was named after Don Pedro de Tovar, the first European to see this astounding chasm after conquering Tusayan (now Hopi) in 1540. Influenced by Nordic and Swiss stone and wood buildings, the hotel exterior was not Pueblo Deco, although the interior hints at this style. A building that is a particular barometer of Colter's interest in Native American design is the 1905 Hopi House, a stepped-masonry structure with an interior decorated with Native American and Hispanic arts and furniture. This building, too, contained a sales area for the Fred Harvey Indian Department.

By the 1920s, Colter was working on El Navajo Hotel in Gallup, La Fonda in Santa Fe, and La Posada in Winslow. She was now a full-time employee of Fred Harvey, and one of the most influential designers of the Southwest—every tourist or traveler staying, shopping, or sightseeing at any location she touched gained a new appreciation for regional art and architecture. The Watchtower at the Grand Canyon is the first manmade structure you see arriving at the South Rim, and it's a masterpiece of Pueblo Deco.

Architect Mary Colter mixed Pueblo masonry techniques with Art Deco sky-scraper decor in the Watchtower, on the southern rim of the Grand Canyon.

OPPOSITE
Actual petroglyphs, or drawings pecked in stone, are mixed into the masonry exterior of the Watchtower.

Hopi Pueblo appears like a mirage from a flat, bleak desert floor. Villages on three mesas are built of the same stone that tumbles over the edges of the cliffs. Multitiered dwellings are reached by steps cut into the sandstone cliffs. Dull beige in the midday sunlight, the villages become luminous at sunset. Altars are scattered about, as subtle as only large boulders situated among other similar rocks can be. If you didn't notice the turkey and eagle feathers tied with cotton string, these altars could melt into the landscape. Looking more closely (but never touching the powerful ritual objects), you can see that the feathers are attached to prayer sticks or *pahos*, which are painted an earthen red. Turquoise color tips the sticks, a color evoking and associated with rain, the most precious resource in an arid land.

A Hopi myth relates their origin: From the deepest recess of the Grand Canyon, a *sipapu*, or small spiritual opening, enabled their people to emerge from the Underworld. Oriented by the sacred peaks of San Francisco to the south, the Hopi ritual cycle begins and ends annually when sacred deities, kachinas, arrive from and then return to the clouds at these peaks. Kachinas express the spiritual facet of the material realm, and their existence is inferred from natural phenomena.

Because of the Hopis' relationship to the Grand Canyon, Colter incorporated aspects of their culture and architecture when she began working on drawings for the Watchtower.

For the form of the building she decided upon the tower. Prehistoric precursors of the Hopi, the Anasazi, had built towers all over the Four Corners area; at Mesa Verde, the Round Tower protects dwellings from invaders. At Hovenweep, also in the region where Utah, Arizona, Colorado, and New Mexico meet, there are towers. Numerous other freestanding ones are scattered about various sites.

These towers served defensive purposes and were used for making astronomical calculations related to rituals and agriculture. The early Hopi archaeologist, Jesse Walter Fewkes, thought they also symbolized Father Sky while the subterranean kivas symbolized Mother Earth, as the two are often found in conjunction.

The Watchtower at the Grand Canyon is built on a concrete foundation with a steel infrastructure reinforcing the walls. It seems to dangle over the precipitous canyon.

You enter via the kiva, now a gift shop, adjacent to the Hopi Room at the ground level of the tower. Every surface of the Hopi Room was painted by Fred Kabotie, a noted Hopi artist, who depicted traditional myths and motifs. The Watchtower is a particularly exciting example of Colter's work. Not only did she use Indian motifs in a manner influenced by the Art Deco movement and transformed by her individual style, but she also wrote a manual for drivers and guides about the process of conceiving, designing, and constructing the building. In it she noted the following:

When it was planned to build a permanent Rest and View House on Navajo Point (now for many years called Desert View), two problems had to be solved in deciding on the architecture. First and most important was to design a building that would become a part of its surroundings—one that would create no discordant note against the time eroded walls of this promontory. Next in importance was to design a building that would make it possible to enhance the *VIEW* from this famous *VIEW POINT*. As its popular name implies, it overlooks the far reaches of the Painted Desert, but it also has the most extensive and spectacular view of the "main" Canyon and of the "River" as it comes down through the Marble Gorge . . .

No conventionalized style of *modern* architecture built of *modern* materials would do this . . . (2)

Colter's tendency to ornament every surface—rawhide-covered handrails, flagstone shelves to hold Indian pots, and wrought-iron light fixtures with stylized Indian motifs, even door handles—was purely Deco.

Kabotie's largest painting in the Hopi Room

THE WATCHTOWER
South Rim of Grand Canyon, Arizona, 1931

illustrates the myth of the Chief's Young Son, who comes to the Grand Canyon to gather salt and pigments (The pigments were used to paint masks and *pahos* which, after being ritually renewed, were used in sacred ceremonies). Fascinated by the Canyon river, he is helped by his father to build a watertight vessel. Floating down the river, he encounters the Snake People and wins the priest's daughter in marriage after taming poisonous snakes through his bravery and magical resources. He and his wife return to Hopi where they settle at Walpi. As Snake Priest,

he introduces the inhabitants to the society's rituals. Rain and the ensuing fertility insure the cult's continuation.

The Hopi Room is covered with other traditional motifs as well, including sun and stars on the ceiling below the first gallery, insects, other motifs related to water, and a large painting of Hay-A-Pa-O, a winged figure underneath a rainbow and cloud motifs. The center of the room contains a wooden case in which a Snake Altar has been replicated. Both Colter and Fred Harvey made a concerted effort to be archaeologically and ethnographically correct in details and information imparted to tourists. On the other hand, most Pueblo Indians are quite reticent about sacred details, so the Snake Altar is probably incomplete.

The first and second galleries above the Hopi Room were painted by Fred Greer and explore prehistoric cave art, murals found in kivas, and other Pueblo paintings. At the first gallery, as you come up the stairs, is a blackened wall with white-etched figures of animals and hunters. It is similar to drawings found in Frijoles Canyon, excavated by Kenneth M. Chapman of the Laboratory of Anthropology in Santa Fe. A bird fetish perches on the balcony.

Colter had a fondness for the Indians' use of stones resembling animals. The stones were carved judiciously to enhance the animal or bird "found" in the stone. Sometimes turquoise eyes were inlaid, and feathers and arrowheads tied to the animal, converting it into a hunting fetish.

She utilized a massive fetish on the exterior which looks like the Great Plumed Serpent, Balolookong. Other paintings in the galleries imitate petroglyphs, while on the exterior, actual petroglyphs are incorporated into the rich surface of the tower. Additional exterior decorative elements include geometrical stacks of stones and zigzags asymmetrically scattered overall.

While the impulse is Art Deco, the lack of symmetry is very Colter. She loved the rough surfaces and imperfections of the handmade and adapted the prevailing aesthetic to her own taste, as is clear in her work, including the La Fonda Hotel in Santa Fe.

Looking up into the galleries of the Watchtower from the Great Room below, one can see constellations and other sky motifs painted by Fred Kabotie on the ceiling. His snake myth painting sits on the lower wall.

The town "Where the West Begins," Fort Worth, once had a wild reputation, suggestive of everything the West could be. Butch Cassidy and the Sundance Kid hid out in "Hell's Half Acre," a sector of saloon-filled streets in what is now the central business district. Cowboys returning from long, lonely cattle drives whooped it up there, carelessly spending money on women, drinking, and gambling. Land speculators, fortune hunters, and bounders of all sorts followed the cattle drives and railroads to Fort Worth. Actually, the sobriquet is derived from an 1843 American treaty with nine Indian Nations defining their territory to the west.

Situated on the bluffs above tributaries of the Trinity River and surrounded by cattle country, the town became a natural focus for expanding railways, including Jay Gould's Texas & Pacific, to transport cattle to abattoirs in Chicago and Omaha. Cattle ranching had become big business by the time of the Civil War. Phillip Ashton Rollins, a cowboy during the last quarter of the nineteenth century, wrote describing the transition of ranching as practiced by the original Mexicans:

To understand this movement and its incentive, one must turn back for a moment to that year 1519 and its Spanish Mexican settlers; and, as with successive generations they numerically increased . . . and spread northward. Each migrating settler took his livestock [long horned Andalusian cattle] with him as he moved. At the end of three hundred years the Rio Grande had long since been crossed, and they firmly established in the southeastern part of present Texas numerous ranches, each covering an enormous acreage and asserting ownership over the great herds that habitually grazed upon it.

The owners of these ranches obtained from them no commercial profit, for the reason that there was no available selling market for their animals.(3)

Rollins was not entirely correct. One of the first

TEXAS & PACIFIC PASSENGER TERMINAL AND WAREHOUSE

1600 Throckmorton Street, Fort Worth, Texas, 1931

cattle drives was made to the West Coast during the gold rush by the Luna family of New Mexico.

Once the Anglo settlers discovered the markets in the East, cattle drives were organized to get the animals to market, where, after the long trek, they had to be fattened first in feedlots. It was only a matter of time before the railroad companies realized that it would be advantageous to run lines into Texas.

The gush of black gold displaced the previous cow town, gilding the city of Fort Worth with a slick veneer of progressive construction and a sprawling urban growth. But it was a while before the nineteenth-century train station was replaced with an edifice befitting the town's new status.

In 1909 the president of Southern Railway addressed a meeting of the American Institute of Architects:

Let us assume that a certain city is provided with station facilities that are not quite up to similar facilities as some other places of approximately the same population and commercial importance. They are not such as the community would like to have, and they are not such as the railway management would consider ideal. The

community believes it is entitled to the best of everything. It does not want a station that will be merely as good as one in a nearby town of the same size. It wants a better one. It would like to have the best and most beautiful station of any town of the same relative importance in the whole section of the country, and it does not hesitate to say so through its municipal officers, its commercial organizations, and its newspapers.(4)

The lavishness and magnificence of the Texas & Pacific Passenger Terminal would seem to indicate that in this instance Fort Worth got what it felt it deserved, the best. There are two entrances to the terminal. One leads to the terminal itself, and the other provides access to the ten stories of office space above the terminal. Both have canopies of aluminum, embossed with zigzags and stylized foliation. The terminal canopy is differentiated by size and decorations on the tie rods, which have stepped pyramids. The doorways to both are of the same embossed brass, but again, the terminal entrance is larger, and the sculpture above the transom windows is more elaborate. An eagle is flanked by stylized compass motifs, zigzags, and foliation.

The entrance for the offices was more overtly influenced by Native American motifs, especially the elaboration and repetition of arrows and stepped pyramids. Diamonds appear in the cast-aluminum spandrels at the terminal level and in brick at each story. Cast-concrete details occur at the parapet, where, as on the warehouse, towers at each corner conceal mechanized functions.

Entering the lobby of the terminal, you are overwhelmed by the encrustation of every surface, light fixture, doorway, and radiator cover. A major theme is the stepped pyramid and this motif is artfully introduced on every surface: enameled cast-plaster-and-brass grilles flank the doors to the concourse, which is similarly ornamented. The ceiling is gold-leafed.

By the time the Texas & Pacific Passenger Terminal and Warehouse was built, the depres-

sion's effects were being felt. The city developed a plan, the Five Year Work Program, in an attempt to delay these effects in the Fort Worth region. The city agreed to raise a bond for supplementary infrastructures associated with the project, and construction of the railroad terminal and warehouse commenced.

The size of the warehouse alone is staggering. It provides 488,000 square feet of warehousing, enabling the tenants to display, refrigerate, and distribute tons of merchandise or commodities to the nineteen railways radiating from what became a central distribution point. In spite of its monstrous size—it measures 611 by 100 feet and has eight stories—the building is elegant. The parapet breaks into five sections, giving some visual relief to the building, which fills an entire city block. It is constructed from reinforced steel and a yellow- or buff-colored brick, favored in Texas over the red brick commonly found elsewhere. Bands of terra-cotta zigzags ornament the parapet sectors, and the corners of the building have towers which conceal the circulation and air-conditioning units. Blue arrows accentuate these towers.

Both the Passenger Terminal and the Warehouse were designed by the chief designer for Wyatt C. Hedrick's firm, Herman Paul Koeppe. Koeppe was a German immigrant who kept in touch with architectural and engineering developments in Europe after studying there in the 1890s. He worked for a short time as an architect for the Santa Fe Railroad's Galveston office. Hedrick established his firm in 1925, opening offices in Dallas, Fort Worth, and Houston. A majority of the buildings produced by the firm in the twenties and thirties were the creative product of Koeppe, who had a strong feeling for Art Deco. His early exposure to German Expressionism and modern tendencies is especially visible. Peter Behrens's factories were influential on the form of the terminal.

In massing and scale, details, and the relation of those to the context of the building and locale, the Texas & Pacific complex is a tribute to the grandeur of the city and to the cultures it moved further west. Replacing the original station, built in 1876 when the T & P first arrived, it reflected all that Fort Worth was and could be.

The ornamented bays of the Texas & Pacific Warehouse relieve the sheer bulk of this block-long storage facility.

The stepped-pyramid motif dominates the radiator grilles, brass ventilation covers, enamelled plaster, and light fixtures of the opulent Texas & Pacific Passenger Terminal lobby.

T he Sangre de Cristo Mountains hover over Santa Fe. In the fall, leaden clouds obscure their peaks, and the air is heavy with moisture. The voluptuous scent of red earth envelops you, floral from the mauve-tinted sagebrush. Colors have a clarity from an earlier rain as shafts of sunlight penetrate the dark sky. Piñon trees are abundant and obscure one's vista, and if there was an adobe on the mesa, it would be difficult to discern. Only the acrid odor of cedar burning provides a clue of anyone else's existence.

Side trips from the station at Lamy, twenty-five miles southeast of Santa Fe, where you could stay at the El Ortiz Hotel, were instantly successful, so much so that within a short time, it made sense to build a spur into Santa Fe. The charm of Santa Fe's environment exerted its influence. Women from Santa Clara or Tesuque could be seen wearing gay ginghams under fringed shawls, strings of turquoise beads, and silver bracelets. Men from Rosario or Arroyo Seco rode into town on horseback with strings of burros loaded with bundles of firewood or blankets woven in Chimayo for sale.

The Palace of the Governors was a delightful variation from traditional civic architecture east of the Mississippi. And the sun was inevitably orange against a sky where clouds meandered. You could wander down unpaved roads lined with cottonwoods and wild flowers, stopping in front of a home with a *nicho*, a recessed space in a wall, devoted to *Nuestra Señora de Guadalupe*, the first New World saint.

For the more adventurous, there were horseback or wagon trips to nearby ruins at Puye, where cliff dwellings were being excavated, or to the turquoise mines near Los Cerrillos, which supplied Tiffany's with this semi-precious stone. A longer trip could be made to the Sanctuario de Chimayo, site of miracles and cures, or to Santo Domingo to see a Corn Dance.

The station designed by Charles Whittlesey isn't far from the central plaza in Santa Fe. Constructed of red bricks but plastered with heavy white stucco on the outside (originally it was brown to resemble adobe), it is a small Mission-

ATCHISON TOPEKA & SANTA FE STATION

Santa Fe, New Mexico, 1909

style building modified by Mary Colter's influence. On the south elevation is a breezeway with stepped or corbeled arches, a feature that is not at all Mission, but reveals instead the influence of Pueblo architecture. A gabled pavilion and a small arcade greet passengers departing from the train. A red-tile roof (now asphalt) overhangs in deep eaves on the east elevation where exposed brackets provide additional support. The gables are decorated with quatrefoils. Later, this motif was replaced by the Santa Fe Railroad's trademark, an encircled equilateral cross. This early building is interesting as an illustration of the transition from Mission to Pueblo styles in the New Mexico region.

Owen Wister wrote about his experience riding the AT & SF in the early 1920s:

Following the tracks of the explorers, the Santa Fe, itself an explorer, most fitly wove the historic association into its life as a modern railway, nourishing itself with what it found in its path . . . it might have constructed Gothic stations, or Greek temples, as well as adapted Spanish architecture— and had it done so, would have been essentially ridiculous.(5)

Fred Harvey and the Santa Fe had found the perfect formula to increase tourism. Realizing that additional services could be provided, Fred Harvey decided to offer a more organized series of tours. Roads improved each year, especially after the First World War. The automobile was becoming an important mode of travel, and the company realized that extensive motor tours would be welcome. Of course, the company still promoted the architecture of the region seen by taking the railroad spur into Santa Fe. A typical advertisement read, '' . . . see the unique adobe flat-roofed houses; the quaint crooked streets . . . ''(6) In 1925 the plan proposed by the director of transportation at Fred Harvey, Major R. Hunter Clarkson, was approved. Formalized tours, the Indian Detours, would be offered in partnership with the Santa Fe.

Patterned after European tours and Erna Fergusson's successful Koshare Tours in New Mexico, these trips would take tourists by the carload or special bus through historic occupied Pueblos and prehistoric sites. Fergusson, who had a graduate degree in history from Columbia University, was hired as the director, and her Koshare Tours were bought out by Fred Harvey.

The female guides were called Couriers, and were required to have college educations, a strong interest in the region, and, preferably, some area of special expertise. Several spoke Spanish either from family or academic education. They wore turquoise or squash-blossom necklaces, velvet skirts patterned after those traditionally worn by the Navajo women, and skirts cinched at the waist with concho belts. A cloche hat was worn instead of a ten-gallon Stetson. A silver thunderbird, the Indian Detours trademark, was pinned to the cloche.

Always in pursuit of authenticity, the Indian Detours imparted historical, archaeological, geological, botanical, and cultural information to tourists. The Couriers' training consisted of a short course given by Sylvaneus Morley, associate at the Carnegie Institute, Dr. Edgar Lee Hewett, director of the School of American Research, and noted archaeologist, Dr. A. V. Kidder.

The male drivers for the Detours were also

The Atchison Topeka & Sante Fe Train Station in Santa Fe reflects the influence of Mary Colter's stepped or corbeled arch designs.

subject to strict requirements, including a minimum knowledge of Spanish, excellent driving skills, and good health. The drivers wore Stetsons and large neckerchiefs, resembling Hollywood cowboys. Loaded into a Packard, the tourist would be treated to interesting lectures and driven in comfort to see the Pueblos and meet the artists who created the pottery, baskets, and jewelry.

Touring cars and buses carried the Indian Detours' emblem, an encircled thunderbird. The vehicles were even painted a special-order color, Tesuque brown, which didn't show the dust as much as other colors. Advertising was directed at passengers on the Santa Fe, reading:

It is the purpose of the Indian Detour to take you through the very heart of all this, to make you feel the lure of the Southwest that lies beyond the pinched horizons of your train window. In no other way can you hope to see so much of a vast, fascinating region in so short a time—and with the same economy, the same comfort, the same leisurely intimacy and the same freedom from all trivial distraction . . . It is 3 days and 300 miles of sunshine and relaxation and mountain air, in a land of unique human contrasts and natural grandeur.(7)

The tours originated in Las Vegas, New Mexico, or Albuquerque, depending on the direction in which you were traveling. Albuquerque welcomed the influx of visitors and their money. Consequently, trading posts sprang up in the central business districts around the railroad station.

MAISEL'S TRADING POST

510 Central Avenue SW, Albuquerque, New Mexico, 1937

Petroglyphs dot the volcanic escarpments. The Rio Grande languidly rambles between the mesas to the west and the Sandia Mountains to the east. Albuquerque is a synthesis of the old and new, having always been a stop along the way. The Hispanic trade route stopped over here, and Route 66 paved the way for tourist-laden cars. Before the advent of automobiles, the train stopped in what became the heart of downtown. Hotels and shops radiated from the train station. The tracks and Central Avenue form the axis. Near Maisel's Trading Post, the great Trost and Trost Hotel Franciscan once stood. People from nearby pueblos regularly came into town to work, sell their pottery and textiles, or pawn silver jewelry.

Maisel's is distinguished by being one of the few Pueblo Deco buildings to employ actual Pueblo and Navajo artists. A linear mural runs the length of the façade and dips into the recessed lobby. The mural, designed and supervised by Olive Rush, a prominent artist of the period who had moved to the Southwest, forms a frieze above large display windows, extending across the façade. Depicting various aspects of ceremonial life, the mural was one of the first to be painted by Indian artists outside the American Indian Art Institute in Santa Fe. Many of the muralists, although students at the time, went on to gain reputations as outstanding artists.

Ha So De painted the *Navajo Ceremonial Hunt*; Theodore Suina the *Corn Maiden*; Olive Rush the *Pueblo Deer Dances, Navajo Mother and Child with Horse,* and *Family in Cornfield*; Tony Martinez painted *Thunderbirds*; Pablita Velarde, *Pueblo Women with Pottery*; Ben Quintana, *Bean Dancers*; Pop Chalee, *Wildlife*; Joe Herrera, *Butterfly Dancers*; Ignatius Palmer, *Apache Dancers*; A Twa Tsereh, *Corn Dance*; and Harrison Begay, *Navajo Yei-bi-chei.*

Mural painting was a technique familiar to Native American artists in the Southwest; kiva murals at Awatobi were used in a ritual context. Animals, plants, and people were elegantly rendered. The Maisel murals are witness to a life force that sustains every medium of Pueblo, Apache, and Navajo art.

This trading post offered other attractions. An interior balcony was provided for tourists who wished to peer down into the basement workshop where Pueblo and Navajo craftsmen fabricated silver and turquoise jewelry. It was exciting to see native craftspeople at work. Jewelry became a stock curio, from copper and brass silver plated pieces made to Fred Harvey specifications (with bows and arrows to signify "Indian") to expensive, finely crafted pieces treasured as heirlooms. The popularity of jewelry was due to its small size—it could be easily packed by a tourist on the road.

John Gaw Meem designed and supervised the building of Maisel's Trading Post. He was the leading proponent of the Pueblo style in New Mexico, creating a visibly different campus for the University of New Mexico. The client for the building, Maurice M. Maisel, told Meem, "that he was not content with the usual Indian thing." Meem goes on to record in his notes, "It was agreed finally that my preliminary study was to be along the lines of a strictly modern structure using where necessary Indian symbols."(8)

Maisel wasn't even content to let Meem determine the plan, and gave him a photograph of a store in Los Angeles, Schaver's, which had a similar recessed lobby but with rounded Streamline corners rather than angular ones. Meem didn't have a tremendous amount of creativity invested in this building, but the decorative touches, which are his, are restrained and graceful.

Framing the entrance are stepped diamonds formed by an aluminum molding. Below the display windows is a band of black Carrara glass etched in silver with a sinuous, faintly floral motif bearing some resemblance to stylized plant forms found on Pueblo pottery. The use of black was no doubt inspired by Maria Martinez, the famous potter of San Ildefonso who worked almost exclusively in black. Aluminum grilles repeat the stepped diamond. A terrazzo floor is decorated with a thunderbird composed of crushed turquoise and coral (recycled waste from the manufacture of jewelry). Silver dollars and Mexican pesos outline various areas of this motif on the floor and spell out the name of the building.

Ten different artists worked on the frieze running across the façade and recessed lobby of Maisel's Trading Post in Albuquerque, one of the few Pueblo Deco buildings to employ Native American artists for its decoration.

(now Office Furniture Mart)
616 Central Avenue SW, Albuquerque, New Mexico, c. 1935

The façade of Wright's Trading Post in Albuquerque, with decoration resembling Santo Domingo mosaic work, is reflective of the Indian jewelry sold within.

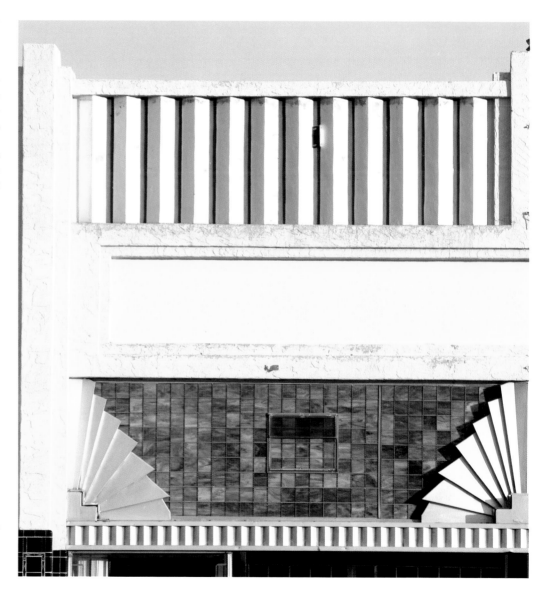

A block away from Maisel's is another early trading post, Wright's. It appears to be earlier than Maisel's and is an imaginative adaptation of Indian motifs that might be attributed to John Gaw Meem. However, records from his office provide no definitive evidence for this conclusion. The recessed entry is flared, and the display windows are surrounded by black- and turquoise-glazed tiles. A band with stepped diamonds appears below the windows beneath the façade, which is divided into three horizontal sections having end piers.

A gently stepped central pier intersects louvered stucco panels reflecting the desert sun. A flat area is framed with stucco, originally containing the name of the building. Below this is a stunning array of turquoise opalescent glass, divided by a central fan of aluminum and flanked by half fans of the same material on either end.

Zuni jewelers still make watchbands and other jewelry using a pavé technique, which is also found on prehistoric Anasazi jewelry. The grid of turquoise is in fact a motif, which translates from the Hopi as, "stacked ears of corn," referring to the effect of row stacked upon row of blue corn. This trading post façade acts as a billboard, advertising Indian jewelry to the tourist.

A photograph of Pueblo mosaic jewelry accompanied an article Kenneth Chapman wrote in 1924 about the Southwest Indian Fair, noting the increasing popularity of anything with Indian motifs: "Pueblo Indians are now producing embroidered fabrics which are in demand for use as table runners, curtains, and other articles of domestic use." He went on to say that the Pueblo jewelers could scarcely keep up with the demand for their work.(9)

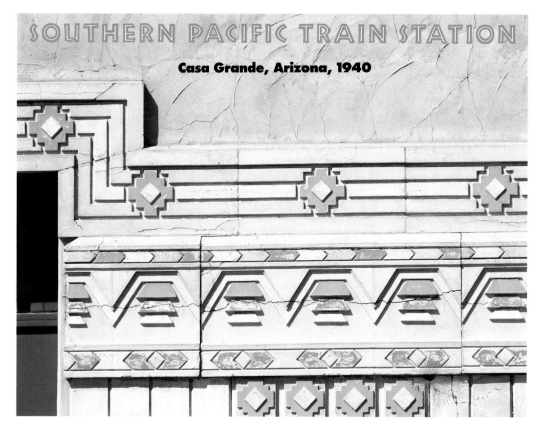

SOUTHERN PACIFIC TRAIN STATION

Casa Grande, Arizona, 1940

Yellow dust blows across the tracks. Somewhere nearby is the first primitive highway to Tucson, where Tom Mix died when his car careened off into the saguaro-studded countryside. The Southern Pacific Train Station now appears to be no more than a flag stop, but its layout and design define it as a larger stop, loading passengers and cargo. Built at a relatively late date, 1940, to replace the one which had burned down two years before, the building is in a reserved Pueblo Deco style, the intervening economic depression having affected the use of costly materials. Glazed terra-cotta has been replaced by colored cast concrete. The station is asymmetrical in both plan and decoration.

A framed stucco structure, the station is low and puebloid, rising two shallow steps from the covered platform on the southern end to the central waiting room. Short, graceless columns support the platform, and the stucco capitals are decorated with motifs that also appear on bands around the windows and doors. The cast-concrete band is grooved and incised with stepped diamond motifs, running arrows, and truncated pyramids. The latter motif, symbolic of cumulus clouds, appears in Navajo sand paintings. During curing ceremonies, medicine men perform rituals using multicolored sands to create intricate patterns on the ground. Sand paintings are erased once the ceremony is concluded. The colors of the cast-concrete were originally bright but under the sun's harshness have faded to softened oranges, turquoises, and yellows. The baggage and cargo were housed on the north end, and that portion of the building is undecorated except for the end of the band and its square volute.

The interior of the lobby has a carved oak band with truncated pyramids and stepped diamonds above the wainscoting. A stenciled cornice at the ceiling uses colors quite different from the outside: cobalt blues, iron-oxide reds, and greens. Again, this band contains another variation of the theme. Interior arches are corbeled.

The perspective was first published in the Casa Grande Dispatch, April 21, 1939, and is signed by the staff architect at Southern Pacific, William F. Meaney. He worked under the chief architect for the railroad, J. Christie. The archaeological Casa Grande is the site of six Hohokam villages and includes a four-story building. If you got off the train here, you knew you were in the heart of "Indian Country."

The fence next to the Shaffer Hotel in Mountainair, New Mexico, is made of cast concrete with

TWO
HOTELS

Perhaps it was the spirit of democracy—anyone who could afford the price of a room should have a taste of luxury. At any rate, hotels, as we know them, were an American innovation. Prior to the establishment of Isaiah Rogers's Tremont House in Boston, you were left to shift for yourself while on the road.

If Fred Harvey revolutionized the quality of food for railroad passengers, Rogers was equally important. He set the standards in how we park our bodies for the night. It's not to everyone's taste to roll up in a blanket and sleep under the stars. Even if you stayed at an inn, rooms were crowded, not to mention beds! Or, you could end up sleeping in the courtyard with carriages and animals. A room to yourself and a lobby to check into did not exist. The lobby was a multifunctional room, primarily a bar. With the 1829 advent of hotels and standards set by the Tremont House came separate rooms, a lobby, service, clean linens, and even soap. Just as every town wanted its own railroad station, every city and town of importance also wanted a hotel.

Rogers's plans and designation of spaces have persisted into the twentieth century. The lobby became the entrance, a formal and gracious public space instead of a bar. Luggage could be left in a separate room, and a newspaper could be read in the library.

Hotels became grandiose palaces for pleasure, transforming travel from a necessary evil into a leisure activity. This attitude extended into steamboat and train travel. The steamboats traveling up and down the Mississippi River were gaudily decorated in white and gold. George Mortimer Pullman decided to design railroad carriages that were more similar to floating river boats than horse-drawn carriages. He added sleeping cars and dining cars, creating a plush environment that invited travel.

Nineteenth-century hotels were initially designed in the Greek Revival style favored by Rogers. Other styles gradually crept in, and by the turn of the century you could stay at the fabulous Tampa Bay Hotel in Florida, its style derived from Spanish Colonial architecture. Fred Harvey, always attuned to the demands of tourism, was the first in the Southwest to build in a regional style (in collaboration with the Santa Fe Railroad). Others soon followed.

Fred Harvey saw the advantages in assembling a system of hotels across the Southwest. Plans were laid for hotels in Gallup, Winslow, and Williams.

Colter's El Navajo preceded Trost's work and may have been influential on his work. She used stuccoed massing to create a structure which was neither indebted entirely to Spanish Mission or to Pueblo architecture. It was uniquely her own style and most definitely a precursor of much of the Art Deco in the West, given its early date, 1923, and especially in view of the fact that the design process commenced during the First World War. As was typical of her creations, it was asymmetrical in plan and form. Fortunately, the La Fonda Hotel in Santa Fe has been fairly accurately conserved in its original condition, so we can see Colter at work, her use of repetition of elements and variation, and her fondness for the rough, worn look of the desert, whether Indian or Spanish in origin.

Henry C. Trost built one of the most distinctive hotels of the 1920s in Albuquerque, the Hotel Franciscan. Wildly influential, it was published in The Architectural Record, among other magazines, and books. Rose Henderson found the interior to have a "sensuous crudeness." In retrospect, her 1927 article, "The Spanish-Indian Tradition in Interior Decoration" can be seen as a definition of Pueblo Deco. Henderson wrote:

The austerity of the general architectural scheme provides an excellent foil for the colored friezes and other decorative details. Richly colored Indian design is effective in dining room ceiling and wall borders and in medallions appropriately set in interesting wall spaces. The design appears on heavy carved ceiling beams and on stained glass windows. It is carried out in vases, flower stands, rugs, hangings, stationery, and other furnishing details. It frames a Southwest landscape painting, a pleasing over-mantel decoration in a room where the main walls are kept severely plain to off-set the dark tiled floor and heavy dark ceiling beams. The whole interior is rich but spacious, filled with fascinating detail that keeps the right accent and is a proper unit with the whole structure.

Mrs. Inez B. Westlake of Albuquerque, who made the designs for the hotel dishes, stationery, and tooled leather furniture, has also adapted Indian decoration for ceilings, panels, bands for pillars and side walls. She gathers her motifs from the work of modern Pueblos as well as from prehistoric baskets and pottery . . . Mrs. Westlake has also used the designs with sympathetic skill for stenciled hangings, embroideries and enamel work.(10)

Although she worked with Michael Holback of Chicago, Westlake was responsible for much of the detail, which was inspired by the Pueblo cultures. So popular was this building that it was featured in The Ferro-Concrete Style, a 1928 book lauding the hotel's plasticity and interior details of concrete, corbeled arches, and niches. Unfortunately, all that remains of this hotel are historic photographs; it's now an empty parking lot.

Mary Colter was kept busy at the Grand Canyon, where she worked on Phantom Ranch, located on the canyon floor. Access was by mule or on foot, and all of the materials for building had to be transported in this manner. The stone cabins and dining and recreational halls are plain, with little decoration. The difficulty of access guaranteed simplicity.

Crazy Horse and Sitting Bull were two of the most famous Sioux warriors fighting the American invasion of the Great Plains during the nineteenth century. Sitting Bull reconciled with the white man and even allowed his photograph to be taken on various occasions. Crazy Horse never surrendered and never allowed "his shadow" to be stolen by the enemy. No image of him exists except in the imagination, ultimately a more powerful medium. His bravery and honor are still legendary.

Every image of a Plains Indian in an eagle-feather headdress symbolizes Crazy Horse's valor. The motif is often used to represent all Indians, regardless of tribe. Even Fred Harvey succumbed. While Indian Rooms at five different train stations in New Mexico and Arizona were selling authentic items by the 1920s, the company wasn't above selling replicas of Plains Indian headdresses and costumes manufactured in Japan. The Plains Nations extended as far south as Texas and northern New Mexico, where they had to compete with indigenous Apaches and Comanches for hunting areas.

Fourteen Plains Indians in war bonnets, each capping a stepped pier, decorate the parapet of the Clovis Hotel. Designed by Robert Merrell before he opened his own architectural practice in Clovis, it was, for a short time, the tallest building in New Mexico, with eleven floors. A simple penthouse is set back above the parapet at the ninth floor. The reinforced-concrete structure is clad in buff brick. The brick contrasts with the cast-concrete piers forming the negative image of the terraced motif. More typical Art Deco floral motifs are incised in the panels.

Two entrances to the north and west are protected by aluminum canopies with stepped brackets. A curvilinear element pervades Merrell's geometrics, including these brackets. (When you see other work of his, such as the Bickley School, it is apparent that he was influenced by the Streamline style, a design style derived from industrial and transportation imagery.) He continued the Indian references on

CLOVIS HOTEL

201 Main Street, Clovis, New Mexico, 1931

the interior. Covering the opening of the hotel in 1931, the Clovis Evening News reported: "In the building, the visitor is greeted by the spacious lobby, with light colored walls, bordered by a wainscoat of elaborately colored tile, worked in Indian design and made comfortable with the finest furnishings."(11) A few wrought-iron light fixtures with arrows and the terra-cotta tiled floor remain, but otherwise the interior has progressively degenerated as the hotel has been sold and resold since the Southern National Hotel Company divested itself of the building.

The Second Street elevation of the original design for the Clovis Hotel is stodgy compared to Robert Merrell's imaginative design, built in 1931.

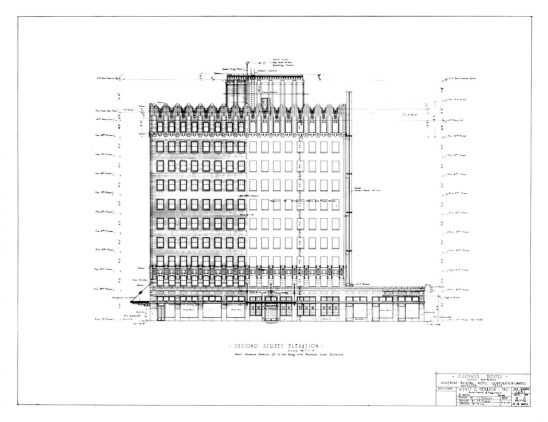

Plains warriors guard the parapet of the Clovis Hotel, a detail which is indicative of the architect's Texas origins.

INSET
This marquee bracket in the Clovis Hotel is an adaptation of the stepped motif in cast aluminum and concrete.

SHAFFER HOTEL

Mountainair, New Mexico, 1928

Clem "Pop" Shaffer must have been the only folk artist working in the Pueblo Deco style. Having had no formal training, he moved out west from Harmony, Indiana, in 1908. Mountainair, the "Pinto Bean Capital of the World," was a stop along the Santa Fe. In 1920, Shaffer began building a hotel and restaurant there. He created a zoo filled with his wood animal sculptures at a site half a mile from the hotel, Rancho Bonito. A 1928 addition he made to the original structure, finished in 1923, is frame and masonry. Including the addition, the hotel contained thirty-three rooms, a lobby, and a restaurant.

Shaffer's facility for carving and painting is most evident in the dining room, where carved and painted vigas alternate with a ceiling painted with serrated diamond motifs. The serrated diamond made its way north from Chihuahua onto the looms of Rio Grande weavers. Cultural exchanges, conscious or not, account for the motif appearing even in Navajo textiles, especially Eyedazzlers, where traditionally, the stepped diamond prevailed. Eyedazzlers derived their name from bright aniline dyes, introduced by traders, producing vivid oranges, purples, and greens, which were then woven in riotous combinations. Pop Shaffer's ceiling is equally colorful.

Shaffer designed and carved elaborate chandeliers for the dining room. The transom windows were created from leaded opalescent glass and spell out *DINING ROOM*; others have thunderbird and tepee motifs. His root monsters were displayed on shelves and mantels. The hotel did well and was a popular stop among tourists. Shaffer's scrapbooks indicate that at its height, as many as 12,000 people annually visited his zoo at Rancho Bonito.

The technique of carving and painting on the façade of the hotel is unusual. Deeply incised or gouged stucco forms geometric motifs and Navajo directional symbols. The incisions are painted various colors. Vigas project at first- and second-story ceiling levels. A zigzag runs along the parapet.

Next to the hotel is a lot where Shaffer's house once stood, and a garden surrounded by a fence with more of his creatures, formed by setting stones into cast-concrete posts and bars. These stone animals might be Shaffer's interpretation of fetishes.

Pop Shaffer was an unusually driven folk artist, aspiring to create an entire universe from hotel to zoo, inhabited by the creatures of his imagination. His awareness of himself as an artist is evident in an autobiography he wrote, in which he notes that when he finished the addition, "In 1929 I built a dining room on the hotel also 8 more rooms the dining room is my unusual piece of work."(12)

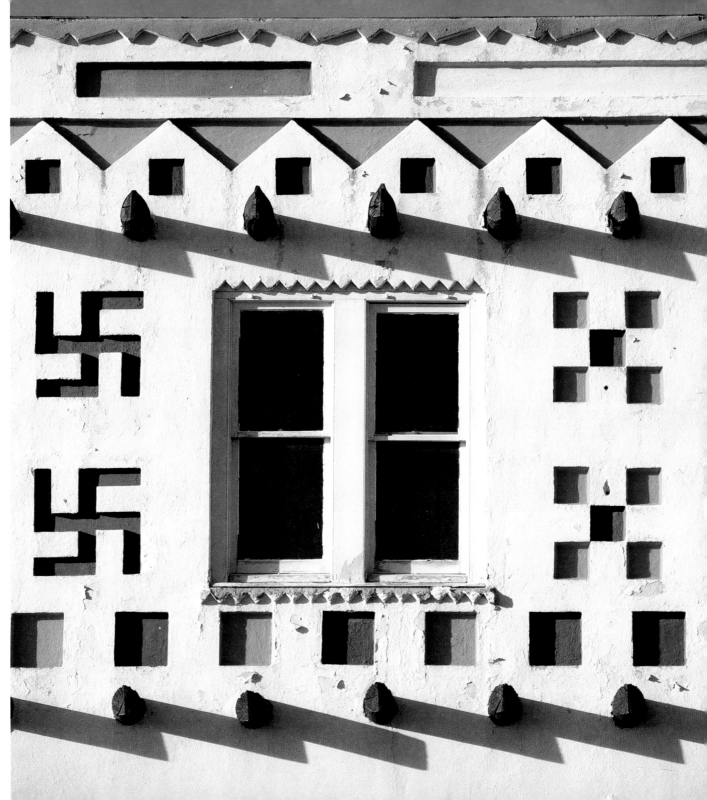

The Shaffer Hotel contains an unusual array of incised and colored stucco decorations, including zigzags, directional motifs, and other geometrics.

Ornate window moldings, a painted wood ceiling cornice, and opalescent glass transoms adorn the Shaffer Hotel's cafe.

OVERLEAF
Clem "Pop" Shaffer had a penchant for carving wooden animals. Here, two of his creations support a curtain rod.

Albert Chase McArthur was in the awkward position of having had to refute Frank Lloyd Wright's claim that he designed the Arizona Biltmore. After selling McArthur patent rights for a textile block, which he never owned, Wright went on to claim design credit for the hotel. It is obvious why he did so. After all, McArthur apprenticed as a draftsman in Wright's Oak Park studio, and Wright was clearly an innovator, using textile blocks as early as 1915 at the Imperial Hotel in Tokyo. Wright must have felt abused: The son of a wealthy family studies with him and ultimately uses the master's ideas and concepts, paying him only a consulting fee. At any rate, McArthur is the architect of record, and the building was published as such in a 1929 issue of *Architectural Record*.

McArthur's relationship with Wright began when his father engaged Wright to design a house in Chicago. After studying at Harvard, McArthur worked in Wright's office in 1907. He left two years later to work for other architects and eventually established his own practice. His brothers had moved to Arizona, and since 1917 they had been interested in constructing a luxury hotel there.

McArthur did tentative work on designs for the hotel, but the project did not crystallize until 1925, when John Bowman, of Bowman-Biltmore, became involved. Having decided to use textile-block construction, and believing Wright owned the patent, McArthur wired him an offer of $10,000. Wright accepted but felt he should come out in the capacity of consultant, which he did, until he was fired four months later. There were accusations of conflicting design specifications. Apparently, Wright countermanded McArthur's directions. Furthermore, Wright was already claiming creative credit. Whatever actually transpired, McArthur must have felt ambivalent toward the man whose creativity was so apparent. By then, it was also determined that Wright did not own the patent for textile blocks, and the Biltmore was later sued by the patent holder.

ARIZONA BILTMORE

24th Avenue and Missouri Street, Phoenix, Arizona, 1929

The textile blocks for the Arizona Biltmore Hotel were created with the help of Emry Kopta, a Hopi sculptor, using a rectangular variation on Frank Lloyd Wright's squares. Opalescent glass, formed in the same manner, was used for light fixtures.

The pattern of the Arizona Biltmore textile block is very different from those used by Wright, and was derived from McArthur's interest in music. He had developed a theory that sound could be visualized as light or actually color frequency. The interference patterns for the G-major and E-minor chords form mirror images. To transform this acoustical concept into production, McArthur worked with the well-known Hopi sculptor, Emry Kopta. The block went on to form the unit for measure, replacing feet and inches. Unlike Wright's square module, this brick measured 18 by 13½ inches. Concrete and glass were molded, and three coordinate systems were used for construction.

The overall design of the Biltmore is indebted to Wright's work: irregular massing, deep shadows, and modulation of light with the patterned bricks. In fact, an article in *Architectural Record* stated that it had been designed "in the spirit of Frank Lloyd Wright's concepts of harmonizing the building with the terrain, . . . of considering as integral parts of the architectural scheme such elements as the furniture, the interior decoration, the system of illumination, and the like."(14)

If McArthur was influenced by Wright, he was equally indebted to Pueblo architecture. The stepped piers to the west of the entrance, the decagonal ballroom, and the stepped corbels in the main lobby can be traced to an awareness of Hopi Pueblo or other similar buildings. The idea for a circular ballroom must have been inspired by kivas, particularly the flattened ceiling and ribbed supports, identifiable with log ceiling supports, or a cribbed technique found in similar circumstances.

Over the years, Taliesin has made additions and remodeled the interior to conform to the spirit of Wright. If McArthur left no other evidence of his skill as an architect, the Biltmore would be even more problematic. There appear to be no other buildings in which McArthur used the textile block. Fortunately, the residences he designed have an individual quality that is less apparent in the Arizona Biltmore.

The Arizona Biltmore
was influenced both
by Wright and by the
Hopi Pueblo—the
ballroom roof is
covered in the same
manner as Pueblo
kivas, with steel
replacing the tradi-
tional wood.

AHWAHNEE HOTEL

Yosemite Village, California, 1927

Yosemite is awesome. Waterfalls seem to leap off 90-degree cliffs. Half Dome is a great hunk of granite shouldering its way into the valley, worn smooth a million years ago by a glacier moving at an eon's pace. The valley it carved out is grassy and lush with a lake so clear it is named Mirror Lake. (The native word *ahwahnee* means "lush valley.") By the mid-nineteenth century, Anglos had reached the area and were so amazed by the landscape that in 1890 Congress preserved it as a national park.

As at the Grand Canyon, a privately held company, Yosemite Park and Curry Co., was concessioned by the National Park Service to build a modern, fireproof hotel in Yosemite Valley. The Park Service owned the land and structure under a renewable twenty-year contract, and set the rates for the hotel. The need for a hotel arose when the Park Service obtained federal funding to pave a highway into Yosemite, allowing the park to be accessible year-round, including the winter.

The Ahwahnee Hotel was not strictly influenced by Pueblo architecture but instead by Mary Colter's designs for Fred Harvey. The most magnificent feature of the hotel is the view from the public spaces of Half Dome, Yosemite Falls, and Glacier Point. It was designed for the landscape by Gilbert Stanley Underwood. A graduate of Harvard's Architectural School, he was the Union Pacific Railway's consulting architect. He was specifically hired because of his previous experience incorporating Southwestern Indian designs into hotels and train stations.

Underwood's design for the Hotel Apache in Yuma, Arizona, had appeared in a book published in the twenties, *The Logic of Modern Architecture*. Illustrating a chapter devoted to "The Fundamentals of Architectural Design Applied

Jeanette Spencer designed the stained-glass transoms and intricate **patterns for the Great Hall's windows and ceiling beams.**

The Great Hall at the Hotel Ahwahnee demanded and received grandiose treatment—tables and chandeliers, all **with Indian motifs, were scattered among Middle Eastern and Navajo textiles.**

to Solving Our Modern Problems," the hotel was used as a successful example of a design that reflects a building's purpose.

It has ever been an established fundamental that the design of a building should reflect the purpose to which that particular building is to be put. This does not mean that the passenger terminal building or an airport should be planned in the shape of an airplane nor that a theatre should be unreal in its design, any more than it means that a railroad station should take the form of a box car or a theatre should be designed by a scenic artist. It does mean, however, that a glance should suffice to allow the observer to recognize at once that an office building is not a cathedral and a bank is not a public library.(15)

The Ahwahnee retains much of its original character, and this is especially evident in the Great Hall, with a massive fireplace at one end and twenty-four-foot-high windows. The transoms are orange, green, and yellow stained glass and were designed by Jeanette Dyer Spencer, a graduate in architecture from the University of California who had studied stained glass at the Ecole du Louvre in Paris. Adapting geometrical motifs from Indian arts, she created magnificent stained-glass panels which give the room an opulence. The ceiling beams are as richly ornamented as the lobby. The hardwood floor is covered with various rugs, and furniture is grouped to give you a sense of comfort. Tables are painted with zigzags. Writing desks, made and painted to the designers' specifications, are placed along the walls. Colonial chairs are interspersed among Tudor pieces. Huge wrought-iron chandeliers illuminate the hall at night.

Spencer worked on the interior with two noted art consultants, Drs. Phyllis Ackerman and Arthur Pope, who selected the textiles, various antiques, and the furniture. Traditional Mexican light fixtures, multifaceted stars, hang in a few areas such as the "roof garden." Navajo and Middle Eastern rugs were tossed over tables and balustrades but are now displayed in cases.

The ninety-two rooms are decorated with stenciled decorative friezes. The mantel over each door is carved with a different Indian design. Everything was barely in place when the official opening celebrations commenced on July 14, 1927. The chef, Felex Teuscher, who had been the chef at Fred Harvey's El Tovar in the Grand Canyon, prepared a sumptuous dinner that included stuffed squab, quenelles, fresh bass, and vegetables. The opening included Harry Chandler, publisher of the *Los Angeles Times*, and "Alphabet" Dohrmann, a San Francisco entrepreneur, but lacked the glitterati later associated with the hotel.

In the twenties and thirties the hotel was host to everyone from Lord Watertree and Eleanor Roosevelt to Charlie Chaplin, Gertrude Stein, and Helen Hayes. Before the official opening, Donald Tresidder, the president of Yosemite Park and Carry Co., distributed a PR statement that was an accurate estimation of the fabulous Ahwahnee: "Built as a monumental structure to conform to the rare charm of Yosemite, it is expected that the Ahwahnee will satisfy the most exacting type of patronage."(17) Even the local Indians seemed pleased when they "saw" in a granite boulder on the southern elevation a fetish of the spirit of Tenaya.

The published design was a six-story puebloid masonry structure. The entrance pavilion was flanked by stylized buttresses, as might be seen on a Franciscan mission church. Thunderbird motifs appear over windows with square headers softened by curves, an effect seen in vernacular adobes when the wooden lintel is rounded by adobe plaster, smoothed by hand and worn by the elements.

It is clear from the construction techniques and uses of materials that Underwood was familiar with Bright Angel. The exterior of the Ahwahnee is faced with granite. Cast concrete, simulating redwood, buttresses, and piers give the surface a heavy texture which contrasts with the polished surfaces of the valley. Balconies, projecting roof beams, and cedar shingles allow the structure to mesh with the forest. If there is any doubt that the exterior was influenced by Colter, one need only look at the interior.

The entrance is reached by passing under a long wooden arcade, decorated with carved and painted Indian designs. The desk area in the lobby has paneling and screens which are also treated in this manner. There is a Spanish feeling to the woodwork, with its curved brackets. The ceiling beams are also heavily carved. Wrought-iron light fixtures integrate Hispanic and Indian elements. Windows stretch from floor to ceiling, offering expansive views.

A long article appeared on the Ahwahnee in the November 1928 issue of *The Architect and Engineer*. The author, Dagmar Knudsen, described the interior:

Your attention is drawn to the beamed ceiling, decorated with many different motifs from California Indian basketry, in brilliant green, orange, reds, and yellows, all colors of the Khilim rugs in the room. This new scheme of decoration which anyone may have if he will but transcribe the designs from the baskets and adapt them to his own ceiling, is carried out in a 10-inch frieze on the greater part of the lobby, leading to and around the main entrance . . . Furthermore, the floor of the wide entrance is inlaid with designs from the baskets of the Pomos, the Hupas, and the Huroks. Henry Howard, after whose plan the mosaic was made, has introduced a new method, both technically and artistically. The designs, on rubber tiles, are cut out like mosaics and set into the acid-stained cement by means of brass strips.(16)

A painted cornice band, cast-iron light fixtures, and a wood screen with scrolled brackets adorn the lobby of the Hotel Ahwahnee.

Soldiers who had served at the Mexican garrison in Santa Fe, immigrants from Spain, and any other Hispanics who were poor or desperate enough, colonized New Mexico after it became known that the region offered no enticing riches. The homesteader would work with his neighbors, pouring mud into forms for the sun to harden into adobe bricks. A small room would be built from these with an earthen floor smoothed with ox blood. There would be few windows, and those would be small, with either panes of selenite or wooden shutters. Doors were made of adzed planks, and heavy log beams, or vigas, supported the ceiling of latias—smaller branches set in a herringbone pattern and covered with brush or cedar bark to keep the dirt roof from filtering through.

As the family grew to include children, in-laws, and the children's families, new rooms would be added, strung in a line or turning at right angles to form L or N shapes. A shed or storage area would be added here, a second story and buttresses for stability there. Only rarely did families band together, building an enclosed plaza, as at Las Trampas. Indian raids were a constant threat, and either single houses or plaza communities were built with defense as a primary consideration. Sturdy walls enclosed interior spaces, kept safe with heavy double gates, or zaguans. High parapets projected above the roof, providing cover for the defender.

Like many adobe structures, La Fonda has been modified over the years. Wings and stories have been added since its construction. No architect or designer has left a greater imprint on it than Mary Colter. The original structure was designed by Rapp, Rapp and Henrickson three years after they had finished the Santa Fe Museum in a style melding the Pueblo and Hispanic building traditions. Fred Harvey acquired the hotel in the mid twenties and Colter was assigned to decorate the interior. She created an enduring atmosphere of comfort. Specific aspects, like the painted window panes, furniture, and walls, now continue as tradition with suc-

LA FONDA HOTEL

100 East San Francisco Street, Santa Fe, New Mexico, 1920 and 1926

ceeding artists repainting the original designs.

At the heart of the lobby is a patio, encased in glass and decorated with gay floral motifs originally painted by Olive Rush. Rush also decorated the larger rooms and suites with murals as well as painting those in the New Mexican Room.

Heavy Mexican furniture allows guests to sit around the portal surrounding the patio or chat around a fireplace decorated with a terra-cotta prayer altar with figures derived from Hopi Kachinas. Wrought-iron hanging lamps have cloud motifs, and in a whimsical mood, Colter designed lamp stands in the shape of yucca and ashtray stands resembling jack rabbits. Every detail was inventive and perfectly executed.

Elevators were installed in the modernization effort, so she designed lintels in the shape of thunderbirds, protecting passengers with outstretched wings. The hallway had painted dados, an undulating curvilinear motif of deep terra-cotta red. Lintels over the guest rooms were also carved and painted with Indian designs. A Nuestra Señora de Guadalupe of Mexican tile graces the wall by the ground floor elevator bank. Tin lamps illuminate the halls, nooks, and niches.

Colter meshed antique furniture from Europe and Mexico with the 798 pieces she designed. Kansas City artist Earl Altaire came to Santa Fe to hand paint every one of the 798 pieces after she had worked out a unique color scheme and design for each of the 156 rooms. Colter was after an aged appearance, and the furniture

was sandblasted to give it a worn veneer. She probably wouldn't have minded guests whittling on the furniture (as they were requested not to do on a Mississippi river boat). "We can't get the mellow effect until things have been used," she is known to have said.(13) Rugs and textiles were trampled by workers in pursuit of this effect, according to Virginia Gratton's wonderful monograph on Colter.

Colter also had no compunction about modifying materials to suit her purposes. Tarahumara pots from northern Mexico were adapted to make lamp bases, with shades made from burlap. She probably preferred these pots to the more intricately painted Acoma or Hopi pots because they were cruder, more obviously utilitarian.

The most attention was given to the guest suites on the fifth floor. All had working fireplaces, balconies, neoclassical antique beds, and other interesting pieces such as antique desks studded with wrought iron, and trasteros, or large cupboards, carved in northern New Mexico. Rush painted various patron saints over the fireplaces, and the feeling is very much like the hacienda of a wealthy landowner.

La Fonda was the perfect headquarters for the Indian Detours. The Couriers lounge had a map of New Mexico painted by Gerald Cassidy, which depicted tour destinations. Lantern slides continuously projected images of Indians, the landscape, and other interesting aspects of the region. Lectures were given in the evening at no charge.

Colter's La Fonda was highly successful, attracting local writers and artists as well as tourists. Her interest in context and regionalism was combined with undercurrents of the Deco aesthetic. Art Deco in the United States was also involved with the issue of context but subordinated this concern to an overall decorative scheme. Repetition and bilateral symmetry were less important to Colter than the vernacular and asymmetry. Not that she was purely a revivalist, but she softened repetitive motifs and elements to create a less self-conscious environment.

This fifth-floor suite in the La Fonda Hotel displays the rough, "lived-in" aesthetic of Mary Colter's designs.

46

The interior of the La Fonda Hotel was transformed according to Mary Colter's specifications — elevators were installed, guarded by Thunderbirds, undulating dados enlivened the hallways, and each door lintel was handcarved.

THREE
THEATERS

Movies were the ritual of the 1920s and 1930s, mesmerizing audiences, allowing fantasy free reign. Special environments enhanced these effects. Movie theaters emulated Moorish palaces, Egyptian tombs, and Mayan temples, and you entered the realm of make-believe as soon as you purchased a ticket. The status of entertainment has always been reflected in the buildings that house this function, and the movie theaters that replaced opera houses, vaudeville, and nickelodeons were no exception.

American theaters were distinguished from their European counterparts by the freedom architects and designers felt to derive inspiration from the New World rather than to re-create and repeat past styles. John Eberson, an Austrian immigrant and originator of the so-called atmospheric theaters, understood this craving for a unique sense of, and expression of, the nation's identity. He found it in the pristine sky of the West, where at night every star could be counted. His first atmospheric theater opened in Houston in 1923, the Hoblitzelle Majestic, now gone. Creating the illusion of clouds obscuring the starlit night instead of an elaborately ornamented ceiling, he instantly created a new trend in theater design.

Eberson's interest in the special characteristics of various regions of the United States led him to capitalize on the Spanish heritage of Florida. Although the 1915 Panama-California Exposition in San Diego had certainly promoted Spanish Colonial and Mission architecture, it was not a nationally popular style for theaters, homes, and commercial businesses until Eberson's fabulous creations in Florida and Texas. Initially his work was a regional response to locale or heritage. Later, the Spanish Colonial and Mission styles were adapted by architects in any region regardless of the context. Those architects unaware of regional styles or appropriate themes could always rely on Mayan or Aztec Revival styles to be both popular and exotic. There were very few truly original regional theaters. Given the fascination with archaeology in the Southwest, it's surprising that so few theaters were built around an Indian theme.

PARAMOUNT THEATER

352 Cypress Street, Abilene, Texas, c. 1932

The Spanish influence on Abilene's Paramount Theater is visible in the large, terra-cotta groupings on the façade which contain references to the conquistadores.

Just as the KiMo in Albuquerque, New Mexico, is a montage of Pueblo culture, the Paramount Theater is the opposite: an homage to the Hispanics who first tamed what is now Texas. George Castle was Abilene's prominent architect during the twenties and thirties. He designed the post office a block away, and all four Deco buildings on the corners of Cypress Street where the theater stands.

Abilene was (and still is) one of those oases of culture for the cowboy—or nowadays the traveler. Chased by rolling black thundershowers, you can take shelter in the movie theater. While it hails hen's eggs and softballs, you can sit under the starry sky of Castle's atmospheric theater, while a projector using hand-colored lantern slides rolls clouds across the ceiling above you.

The exterior is of buff brick, with large-scale terra-cotta details judiciously placed at the parapet, which is scalloped and flanked symmetrically by larger scallops and false balconies. Panels containing coats of arms alternate with medallions containing a conquistador's paraphernalia: helmets, swords, and other elements. The medallions and coats of arms are set on backgrounds of blue terra-cotta with white curlicues and details.

Castle's use of large motifs is atypical of terra-cotta detailing. Small elements were generally used to create large patterns. The terra-cotta contrasts with the broad expanse of buff brick and a vertical marquee. Engaged piers and smaller blue medallions are now partially obscured by the later marquee, but the interior has been restored to its original condition.

Voluptuous gilt and red plush envelop you after you purchase a ticket at the blue-and-white-tiled ticket booth. An arcade encircles the lower lobby, where statues, paintings, and furniture give the theater a warm feeling. Enameled stucco walls are roughly textured and contrast with gilded capitals above smooth piers. The vigas are heavily decorated with geometrical motifs, the result of Hispanic influence, although there are curvilinear elements similar to those found on Eastern Woodland Indian beadwork.

The theater itself is designed to impart the feeling that one is in a Spanish or Mexican plaza at night. The stucco walls resemble adobe. Balconies and exterior windows, which appear lit from within, are scattered about. When the lights are dimmed, and the magic lantern produces its atmospheric effects, you can image you are listening to flamenco guitar and breathing the perfumed desert air.

KiMo THEATER

The KiMo Theater was conceived by an Italian immigrant, Oreste Bachechi, as an homage to his beloved Southwest. He was determined that the architects, Robert and Carl Boller, would construct "America's Foremost Indian Theater." As patron, Bachechi had insisted that Carl Boller and Carl Von Hassler travel about the state to become imbued with its cultures. A weather-beaten trader, known only as Schmidt, was architect Carl Boller's guide. Accompanied by the artist Carl Von Hassler, they re-traced routes Schmidt had trekked while trading furs years earlier. They visited Truchas and other small Hispanic villages huddled about churches—masses of adobe with buttresses and symmetrical forms. San Felipe and Santo Domingo Pueblos were en route. There the architect could see asymmetrical urban dwellings as well. Taos Pueblo, re-created by Von Hassler on the walls of the foyer of the KiMo, is at the base of the Sangre de Cristos, site of sacred mountains and lakes, and was their final destination. Inez B. Westlake, already noted for her work with Trost and Trost on the Hotel Franciscan in Albuquerque, worked with the Bollers on the interior design which was complemented by murals painted by Von Hassler.

Quintessentially Pueblo Deco, the KiMo is constructed of reinforced brick heavily stuccoed to resemble adobe plaster and slathered with terra-cotta ornament. Westlake had a fondness for the shield motif, which she derived from the great Hopi potter, Nampeyo, and used in the Franciscan. Bands of shields alternating with elaborate spindles run above the third-story windows on a tripartite façade. The shields are decorated with a Pueblo rain motif, loosely describing cumulus clouds with rain streaks, alternating with the Navajo directional motif and a bird motif from Acoma pottery. A running stepped pyramid links the spindles and frames the upper portions of the shields. When corre-

The KiMo, "America's Foremost Indian Theater," was originally designed as a stage venue, but was adapted for film by the thirties.

BACHECHI·THEATRE·ALBUQUERQUE·N·M—BOLLER·BROTHERS·ARCHITECTS·LOS·ANGELES·CAL·&·KANSAS·CITY·MO

sponding with piers, the shields cascade down in diminishing steps composed of triangles, chevrons, and stylized feathers.

Photographs from the twenties of Indian ceremonial parades in Albuquerque show numerous participants carrying such shields decorated with feathers and other appendages. There was apparently sufficient interest in this motif at the time to warrant a Fred Harvey brochure entitled *The Hopi Sun Shield: Its Meaning.*

The band of terra-cotta shields continues over the three windows on the west elevation, which is relieved of its massive quality by indented forms resembling balconies or other adobe modeling. Two sets of shields are connected by zigzags of red-, white- and blue-glazed tiles. On both this elevation and the façade there is a visual flow. The ground-floor windows are framed by corbeled arches, a motif that is repeated in a smaller scale at the spandrels between the second- and third-floor windows. On the first level, the stepped arch is filled in with painted spindles, and at the spandrels with a checkerboard motif, symbolic of corn in Pueblo mythology. Stout pilasters with terra-cotta capitals of frets and volutes divide the first-story display windows; in the corner a cafe was once located. Kachina masks of salt-glazed tiles appear below the capitals.

Copiously tiled, the foyer is also heavily frescoed with trompe l'oeil scenes of a pueblo, decidedly Taos. The ticket booth is embellished with multi-colored glazed tiles with running arrow motifs and large, decorative terra-cotta tiles. These large tiles have Mayan overtones. The terraced motif is repeated in ceiling details, tiles, doors, murals, and arches.

Inside, wrought-iron water birds strut along the stairs and mezzanine. The stairs' walls have murals depicting the mythical "Seven Cities of Cibola." Glowing with eerie effect, cow skulls illuminate the lobby, mezzanine, and interior of

the theater. The shield motif is repeated in the theater, alternating with cow skulls to form a cornice. The ceiling has concrete beams painted to resemble wood and decorated with animals and geometric motifs. The highly decorated proscenium and flanking corn altars are now gone as the result of fire and changes made to accommodate the movies that displaced live theater, but the KiMo remains a tribute to the Indian and Hispanic cultures. Pablo Abeita, a friend of Bachechi's from Isleta Pueblo, expressed the theater's magnificent attributes when he named it. The KiMo truly is the "King of its kind."

OPPOSITE FAR LEFT
Every detail of the KiMo is inspired by Native American arts—the door handles are kachinas, mural frescoes line the walls, and terra-cotta tiles encrust the ticket foyer.

OPPOSITE LEFT
The Pueblo shields on the KiMo's west façade are framed by stepped pyramids, elaborate finials, and red, white, and blue terra-cotta zigzags.

RIGHT
The KiMo's mezzanine is embellished with vibrant polychrome terra-cotta cow-skull light fixtures, and wrought-iron balcony supports in the form of water birds.

COURT HOUSES AND PUBLIC BUILDINGS

Like commercial buildings, public buildings must convey a symbolic message. If the building is a courthouse, the message is serious, marking those occasions when you use the legal system to ritualize personal or social events or to obtain justice, and conversely, when the system itself pursues criminal justice.

The commercial building's focus is its façade, but the public building is treated more three dimensionally, and it often has several entrances. Each entrance may signify a different purpose. For instance, the jail may be accessed by a small entrance. The general public may enter via a main lobby in order to register deeds or file lawsuits.

People out West instinctively realized that a Second Empire courthouse or a Gothic school was not especially expressive of the region. Breaking physical ties with older, established urban regions enabled the pioneers to embrace new concepts regarding architectural expression of culture and region. Many of the buildings built with either state or federal funds tended to depict the Indians and cowboys, the Spanish and Anglos, cattle ranching and oil strikes.

After the First World War, a Public Buildings Commission was appointed to advise Congress on the administrative space needs for the expanding and increasingly departmentalized government. The commission discovered that there was a need for a new type of building, simply termed a *federal building*, which could house numerous federal divisions under one roof. Additional courthouses were needed, as the legal system added appeal levels and other departments. The commission decided that the decisions regarding location and construction of federally funded buildings should be made on the basis of "business considerations" rather than the usual political bias. As a result, the Public Buildings Act was passed in 1926. Spending was increased during the following years until 1933, when the program was supplanted by the New Deal and its Public Works Administration (PWA).

James E. Wetmore, the Acting Secretary of the Supervising Architect's Office in the Treasury

A cowboy riding a bucking bronco symbolizes the rodeo so many gather to watch at the Will Rogers Memorial Auditorium within.

Department at this time, was not an architect. Starting his career in Washington, D.C., as a stenographer, Wetmore later attended George Washington University to obtain a law degree. His work as Supervising Architect was in a purely administrative capacity. He felt strongly that de-

signs should be appropriate to the region, and encouraged designs incorporating regional symbolism. At the same time, these buildings had to organize space to accommodate various work functions. Wetmore favored modernism's open interior space planning, but preferred a beaux-arts formalism on the exterior with a central entrance and bilateral symmetry. Even in the Southwest, where the modernist use of asymmetry had been preceded by a similar result in vernacular buildings, public buildings designed by the architects in the Office of Treasury under Wetmore's supervision were strictly formal.

Paul Phillipe Cret's work during this period exerted an influence on architects working for the federal government by adapting modern materials and techniques to classicism. This stripped-down classic style became favored for any building with a government function. Cret's 1932 Folger Shakespeare Library in Washington, D.C., had the strongest impact. Reverberations could be seen as far away as the Will Rogers Memorial Center in Fort Worth, Texas. Bertram Goodhue exerted a similar influence from the West Coast.

In 1939, C. W. Short and R. Stanley-Brown published a survey of public buildings funded by the PWA. The PWA had changed since the Public Buildings Act. It had become a financial institution, and the authors describe how it worked:

The PWA does not design any buildings or projects. It does not write the specifications or make any drawings. The character of architecture, the materials to be used and the type of construction are left entirely to the private architects and engineers employed by the owners on Non-federal projects and those employed by the Federal agencies on Federal projects. The PWA acts somewhat in the nature of a bank or a large building and loan association.(18)

Since unemployment was one of the major economic issues during the depression, the focus of the PWA had changed from simply constructing buildings for the government. The government was now to subsidize the construction of buildings for public purposes in order to increase the range of construction and, consequently, employment. Schools, hospitals, and armories could be built with PWA funds. Additionally, the design process no longer originated in Washington; local architects were utilized instead. When an application was made for funds, it had to include the proposed solution for a specific lack of facilities—such as hospital, auditorium, or museum—the estimated cost, plans, and descriptions of materials and construction. This new direction of government building encouraged the use of local, inexpensive materials, since cost was definitely a factor. Local craftspeople and artists were engaged to decorate these structures. As a consequence, regional attitudes towards civic architecture emerged.

Financial allotments could vary for a nonfederal project requesting a loan for up to fifty-five percent of the total and a grant from the government for the remainder. A federal building could receive a grant amounting to one hundred percent of the cost. Many of the courthouses in the Southwest were built under this program.

Small communities in agricultural or ranching regions could finally build much-needed facilities. Robert Merrell's courthouse in Portales, New Mexico, was built using cast concrete and aluminum. His design is an elegant solution with regional overtones—a cast-concrete frieze of cowboys riding across the façade. Spandrels are decorated with the state symbol, a Zia sun. John Gaw Meem, one of the most eminent architects in the Southwest at that time, designed the Pueblo Revival hospital for the Veterans Administration in Albuquerque. Carson City, Nevada, built a state supreme courthouse, while a museum was built to house an art collection for Wichita, Kansas.

Architects were rarely selected by competition; instead, a local architect was selected on the basis of previous work and reputation.

Short and Stanley-Brown stated in their survey:

The PWA programs afforded to many of the architects and engineers employed by non-federal public bodies, their first opportunity to do work in which the Federal Government was interested, even though indirectly. The psychological effect of this, on the whole, was to cause them to produce the best work of which they were capable. The resulting improvements in planning, construction, and design were appreciated by the public bodies who employed them, thus bringing about an advance in the requirements of quality in public buildings. Naturally, this applies much more to the rural districts than to cities where the standards were already high.[19]

In fact, many rural areas had talented architects, but the quantity of work was a limiting factor, as someone of Merrell's or Guy Carlander's talents prove. From 1933 through 1939 there were seven regional PWA offices to correspond with the associated segments of the country. The authors noted regional differences and the impact the program had on design:

Region No. 5: This region contains the States of Louisiana, Oklahoma, Arkansas, Texas, New Mexico, Colorado, and Kansas, covering an area of 746,534 square miles. The climate varies from semitropical on the Gulf coast to severely cold in winter in the mountain regions. As a result, the native styles of architecture show a wider variation than in any other region. Much interesting work, influenced by the Indian adobe architecture, has been done in New Mexico. The work in Texas and Louisiana shows the influence of the Spanish and French traditions.

Climate has been the controlling factor in the development of plans. In the coastal regions southern exposure to take advantage of the Gulf breeze is of primary importance. In New Mexico, Colorado, and northern Texas, small windows and thick or well-insulated walls must provide protection against the heat of the sun in summer and the extreme cold in winter. Such varying conditions of climate have resulted in a considerable variety of plans.

Much of the building material used in the region is produced locally. Brick, clay products, limestone, marble, granite, lumber, hardwoods, and cement are all available. Most metal products and steel must be brought from other States.

Region 6: The States of California, Utah, Nevada, and Arizona are included in this region, which is climatically divided into the northern and southern sections differing completely from each other. It has an area of 467,933 square miles. Most of the buildings in Utah, Nevada, and Arizona do not show very great advances in design but in California it is fair to say that almost a new school of architectural design has been evolved. The "Field Bill," enacted in the State legislature following the earthquakes of 1933, and discussed in Chapter Four of this volume, was primarily responsible for this. It caused the abolition of all types of veneer construction and the elimination of projecting cornices and free or loose ornamental features.[20]

There were forty different departments, bureaus, and agencies involved with the construction of federal buildings under the PWA, but the greatest number—primarily post offices and courthouses—were constructed by the Treasury Department. The Federal Building in Albuquerque was built under this program, as was the post office in Gallup, New Mexico. The Panhandle Plains Museum in Canyon, Texas, was one of the few exceptions. Half of the total building cost of $55,000 was funded by public subscription—a tremendous amount of money given the rural nature of the town and the depression economy. But all of the buildings in this chapter are regionally based in either ornament or form, and all have been touched by the Art Deco aesthetic.

The courthouse was designed by W. C. Townes's firm, Townes, Lightfoot and Funk, and, like many architects working on civic buildings at the time, they were concerned with making it regional or contextual. A simple way to introduce such references was through the use of symbolic figures. The regionalism of courthouses was concurrent with a search for "Americanism." In fact, it was this search that led to a greater appreciation of one's region and culture. As the movie industry had already discovered, cowboys and Indians captivated audiences, so if you were fortunate to be in an area that had witnessed this phenomenon, why not capitalize on it?

Townes embellished the two façades with a braided Indian wrapped in a blanket, facing a leather-clad frontiersman carrying a rifle—one pair per façade. These terminus figures, Indian and Anglo, coincide with piers and are very geometric and schematic. The lower quarter of the figures disappears into the plane of the terracotta pier. Smaller piers decorated with local vegetation intervene between the figures at the top of this eight-story structure. One entrance is major and more heavily decorated; it is accessed by a formally landscaped path. The other entrance faces the street, giving the police who use the jail facilities easier access.

Like many commercial and public buildings of the time, this one steps up in a series of deeply accented setbacks, not really necessary in terms of zoning, given the site: an entire city block surrounded by wide streets and low buildings. A triple-arched pavilion leads into a recessed entry under a Texas longhorn steer cast from aluminum. Elongated light fixtures hang over the entrance.

A terraced pyramid above the central arch is decorated with an interesting terra-cotta motif of prickly-pear cactus in bloom surrounding a yoke. The architect was alluding to the Texas Panhandle, which is covered with cacti, but it's also possible that Townes had read Paul T. Frankel's 1928 book, *New Dimensions: The Decorative Arts of Today in Words and Pictures.* Below a photograph by Ralph Steiner of a tall

POTTER COUNTY COURTHOUSE

511 South Taylor Street, Amarillo, Texas, 1932

ABOVE
Cast-aluminum longhorn steers appear on both the east and west entrances of the Potter County Courthouse.

fluted cactus casting a shadow from a narrow window Frankel had written, "The cactus has established a very definite place for itself in modern art because of its simplicity of line, its interesting silhouette and relation to modern form."[21]

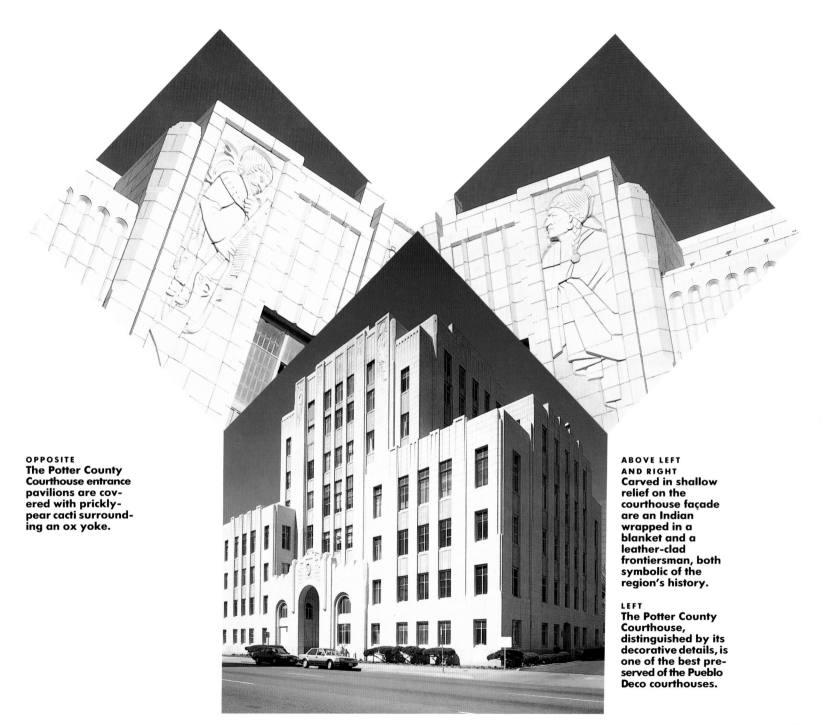

OPPOSITE
The Potter County Courthouse entrance pavilions are covered with prickly-pear cacti surrounding an ox yoke.

ABOVE LEFT AND RIGHT
Carved in shallow relief on the courthouse façade are an Indian wrapped in a blanket and a leather-clad frontiersman, both symbolic of the region's history.

LEFT
The Potter County Courthouse, distinguished by its decorative details, is one of the best preserved of the Pueblo Deco courthouses.

The entrance to E.F. Rittenberry's Panhandle Plains Museum is a rich tableau of natural and man-made history.

A running frieze of prickly pear is above this ferocious wolf's head, one of many sculpted animal heads on the museum's façade.

DEDICATED TO THE PIONEERS

STATE OF TEXAS
ROSS S. STERLING
GOVERNOR

BOARD OF REGENTS
A. B. MAYHEW
HENRY PAULUS
WILL HAYES
THOMAS H. BALL
J. W. FITZGERALD
JOHN E. HILL
H. L. KOKERNOT
W. G. CRANE
WEBB WALKER

J. A. HILL
PRESIDENT OF THE COLLEGE

RITTENBERRY & GARDER
ARCHITECTS

W. FRANK LITLE
CONTRACTOR

The Panhandle Plains Museum is situated in the general vicinity of the trail Charles Goodnight used to herd 1,600 cows from Colorado to found a ranch on the Llano Estacado in 1876. He entered Palo Duro Canyon using Comanche trails. Having moved out West with his parents when he was eight years old, he grew up hunting with Caddo Indians, learning to read trails and to exist with a minimum of resources. Goodnight later fought the Comanches and Kiowas to supplant their hunting lands with cattle ranges. Eventually, with a partner, John G. Adair, he expanded his holdings to a million acres and more than 100,000 head of cattle.

Ranching practices were quickly modified by the intruding Anglos. The Mexican ranchers were neither as acquisitive nor as assiduous in protecting their herds, and stories abound of Anglos who weeded out unmarked cattle to brand them with their own insignia. Branding, or burning a mark with a hot iron onto a critter's hide, was introduced by the Spanish, who had elaborate, sinuous markings. The names for brands are sometimes as fanciful as the marks themselves: Lazy S (lying down), Flying X (wings attached), or Rocking K (a rocker under the K).

The architect of the Panhandle Plains Museum, E. F. Rittenberry, was cognizant of the area's history and the importance of cattle before the oil strikes. The entrance to the museum is dominated by a decorative panel around the portal. Against a background of squares outlined in rope is a full-grown Texas longhorn steer. The squares each contain a local brand: Flying U Bar, Diamond C, Lazy U Bar, and Crazy S with a Barb.

The entry is flanked by grooved piers, each decorated with a figure. A cowboy faces a Comanche warrior. Sculpted eagles project from either side of the modified entablature. In January 1933, the Amarillo newspaper described the entrance:

The highly decorative stone carvings displayed on the front of the new museum

PANHANDLE PLAINS MUSEUM

Canyon, Texas, 1932

building of the Panhandle Plains Historical Society represent more than just an attempt at architectural ornament and design. The inlaid plaques and the relief carvings constitute a virtual museum within themselves, depicting very graphically the glamorous history and picturesque natural inheritance of the plains country.

The carvings were executed by the sculptors of the Texas Quarries, Inc., of Austin. Actual photographs taken of native fauna and characteristic scenes were used to guide the stone-carvers in their work. Forms of Wild Life—Just beneath the ornamental fineal belt on the facade of the new structure are four inland plaques, two on either side of the front entrance, representing the most characteristic forms of wild life in this section. These carvings, constructed so as to give a side as well as a front view, are of a jack-rabbit (sic), an antelope, a buffalo, and a lobo wolf.

Around the main entrance of the building is grouped a series of carvings which further develop the historical motif. Guarding the entrance on the corners of the portal projection are two giant eagles. Closer to the door are imbedded two huge slabs representing in relief the two first citizens of the great plains, the Indian and the cowboy. Immediately around the door are represented in glazed sandstone more than a hundred of the famous cattle brands of West Texas.(22)

The massing of the building is designed symmetrically with the entrance foremost or projecting out from the flanking wings, which are stepped back again to a third setback without any windows. The vertical windows on the second phase of the wings have cast-concrete panels below, which depict the early cattle trails and the settling of the area. The ends of the wings are flanged and have grooved piers. The parapet of the building is decorated with a running prickly-pear cactus motif which is strikingly original.

Carved limestone
panels, with an
Indian and a
rancher in strong
relief, set off the
museum entrance,
above which
are carved the
cattle brands of
local ranches.

Ornate bronze light fixtures illuminate the museum's entrance at night.

UNITED STATES COURTHOUSE

501 10th Street, Fort Worth, Texas 1933

The architect of the United States Courthouse, Paul Cret, was one of the preeminent architects of federal buildings and monuments in the 1920s and 1930s. Cret was largely responsible for and associated with a streamlined classicism which has been termed "starved." The style emphasizes volumes rather than applied decoration, and axial spaces with grand entrances. Cret taught at the University of Pennsylvania for thirty-four years after arriving in the United States in 1903 from France. His career has an unexpected aspect: for a very short time, his work reflected Native American culture.

During the early 1930s he was associated with the Chicago designer, S. B. McDonald, and the Santa Fe Advertising Manager, Roger W. Birdseye. Their project encompassed the design of five different interiors for an equal number of Pullmans, and interiors for a dining car and a lounge car for the new Super Chief, the fastest transcontinental railroad service at that time.

Each of the Pullmans was named after a Pueblo, including the Isleta, the Orabi, and Taos, and all had ivory ceilings and were lavishly panelled with exotic wood veneers: rosewood, ebony, and teak. The color schemes were typically Southwestern: iron-oxide reds, turquoises, and beiges. The lounge car, the Acoma, was painted in orange, beiges, brown, and blue—that cobalt color of the Southwestern sky. A Navajo rug lay on the floor.

Mary Colter was charged with designing the place settings for the dining car, and having recently seen examples of Mimbres pottery being excavated from sites in southern New Mexico, she chose this as her inspirational source. She made thirty-seven variations of motifs using geometrical and pictorial elements found in the sophisticated pottery produced by the Mimbreno Indians. The Syracuse China Company produced the ware.

Photographic murals and Navajo sand paintings completed the decorative schemes. The luxury and speed records set by the Super Chief made it an instant success, especially with the Hollywood crowd.

When Cret designed the courthouse in Fort Worth, his working knowledge of Indian motifs was related to this experience. In terms of massing, the courthouse is simple, with only one stepped-back level, the uppermost (fifth) floor. The second, third, and fourth floors are articulated by angled windows which create a three-dimensional zigzag, a rather innovative interpretation of this motif. Spandrels of cast aluminum separate the second- and third-story windows. The motif in the spandrels is also a Cret innovation, and ambiguous. It could be a stylized fret with an elongated stem, or perhaps a T, for the courthouse does stand in Tarrant County.

The main entrance faces north and is wide and enveloping, in contrast to the more intimidating vertical entrances Cret used on other buildings in Washington, D.C. A scalloped frame of cast aluminum surrounds each of the portals, and cast-aluminum transom grilles form the lower half of stepped diamonds. The elements are hatched in a manner reminiscent of a feather, and each step is elongated further with an arrow. Variations of these elements are found on the torchère that flank each doorway. Considering the other buildings Cret designed in Texas, including those at the University of Texas in Austin, this courthouse is a unique tribute to the native cultures displaced by ranchers and oilmen.

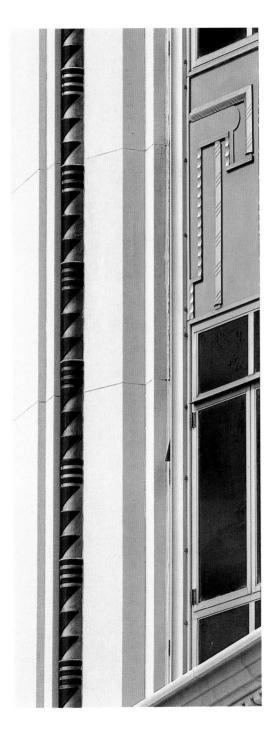

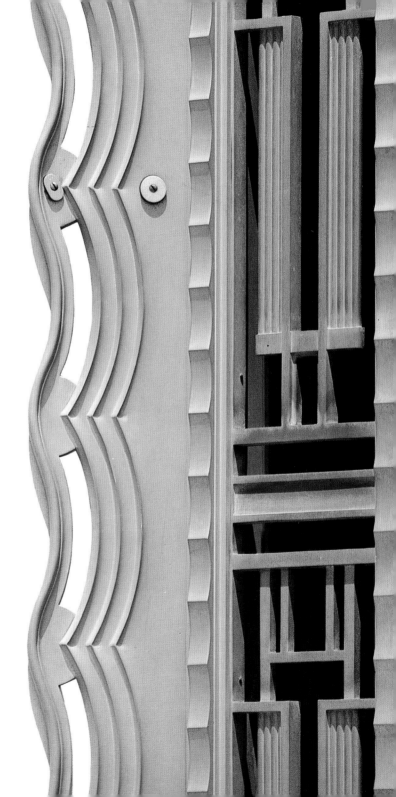

OPPOSITE
The stepped-pyramid transom grilles on the entrance to the United States Courthouse in Fort Worth are rare deviations from architect Paul Cret's "starved classicism."

LEFT
A three-dimensional zigzag motif outlines the fenestration of the second, third, and fourth floors of the courthouse.

RIGHT
The doors of the courthouse are elegantly framed by scalloped molding—a Hispanic motif.

The tile frieze on the façade of the Will Rogers Memorial Center in Fort Worth portrays the industrial growth of Texas in the twentieth century.

Texas celebrated its Frontier Centennial in 1936. This group of buildings was constructed for the livestock shows associated with the Centennial's fiestas and exhibitions, most of which occurred in Dallas. The center was built with financing from different sources. The city of Fort Worth made the largest allocation. Money was also obtained from the PWA and the United States Centennial Commission.

The remainder of the funds was raised by Amon G. Carter through a network of local contributors. Carter, by the 1930s, was a powerful force in Fort Worth. Arriving in the early part of the twentieth century, he worked initially as advertising manager for one of the city's newspapers, eventually buying out a William Randolph Hearst paper in order to start the *Star Telegram*. He expanded his media base to encompass the emerging radio technology, creating the city's first radio station in 1922.

Through the media, he became a great friend of the cowboy humorist from Oklahoma, Will Rogers, who regarded Fort Worth as his second home. When Rogers was killed in an airplane crash in Alaska, Carter was determined to name a lasting memorial after him, and this center is a wonderful tribute.

Pioneer Tower can be seen from a distance, a counterpoint to the low, rounded façades of the coliseum and auditorium. It is grooved at the corners and steps up in successive layers near the top. Cast-concrete steps at the corners form the decoration of this brick pinnacle. The interior has historical plaques and a sculptured bust of Will Rogers.

From the front, both the auditorium on the west and the coliseum on the east have the appearance of curved wings, but the coliseum is infinitely larger. Both façades have long tile murals above the entrances, designed by the project designer, Herman P. Koeppe of the Wyatt C. Hedrick firm. On the auditorium façade, a mural traces the industrial development of the region while above the coliseum entrance another mural depicting the settlement of the West pushes across. The Indians portrayed all wear

WILL ROGERS MEMORIAL CENTER

3301 West Lancaster Street, Fort Worth, Texas, 1936

The use of glass bricks, bulky volumes, and simple details on the entrances to the center reflect the waning of the Pueblo Deco style in the face of demanding economics and the rise of the International Style.

feathers and are shown to be hunting and working peacefully, with tepees in the background, as well as that ubiquitous symbol of Texan pride, the Alamo. Frontiersmen and settlers are shown trading with the original inhabitants. None of the violence associated with the actual process is implied. The social realism style of the mural, endorsed by the WPA, did not extend beyond an idealized reality.

The same can be said for the mural over the auditorium. The industrialization process is depicted as serene. Architects and builders with plans work with laborers to build skyscrapers and oil rigs. Airplanes and other technological innovations fill the background. The murals were produced by the Mosaic Tile Company of Zanesville, Ohio, and form appropriate friezes for a Pioneer Centennial celebration.

The impetus for this complex was Art Deco, but it was clearly stifled by the Streamline aesthetic dominant in the thirties. Cret and Goodhue had begun to make their influences felt, too. Grooved piers, a mannerism associated with each of these architects, separate the five entrances (for each structure). Attenuated glass-brick transoms above the doors are decorated with aluminum vegetal motifs and stepped granite lintels. The cast-aluminum details are, in tech-

nique, very much like those on the United States Courthouse in Fort Worth built three years earlier. On the east elevation of the coliseum are cast-concrete panels of cowboys breaking broncos against a desert landscape.

Hedrick had a talent for assembling teams of creative people, and, in the coliseum, he found an engineer who proposed a novel solution for construction of the large dome without supporting columns. Using the concept of compression, Herbert M. Hinckley, Sr. designed steel trusses that met in the center of the dome. The lobby's decoration is restrained. A stenciled band encircles the mezzanine with additional attention to the area coinciding with the piers. Indian motifs are integrated with foliation, but the leitmotif of the interior (and the complex as a whole) is the terraced pyramid and diamond, appearing in brass light fixtures, arches leading to other areas of the complex, and ultimately, the tower.

Named after the noted Oklahoma humorist, the Will Rogers Memorial Center was constructed for the Frontier Centennial festivities of 1936, and represents the transition from Deco to Streamline styles.

700 Main Street, Clovis, New Mexico, 1936

In the beaux-arts tradition, after finishing an advanced architectural degree at Texas A & M, Robert E. Merrell traveled around Europe, Mexico, and the West Indies during the early 1920s. After assimilating historical styles and the exciting new work being done by Peter Behrens and Walter Gropius in Germany, he returned to Texas.

He was chief draftsman for Levesay and Weideman in Beaumont, who were retained by the Southern National Hotel Company in Houston to erect a new hotel in the heart of cotton country in New Mexico: Clovis. In his dual capacity as designer and inspector of construction, he frequently traveled to this small town, and when he decided to set up his own practice, he moved there.

Merrell specialized in commercial work (One of his first jobs after moving was the Pueblo Deco-style Bickley School in 1932.) and designed the courthouse in a style identifiably his own. He rarely imitated historical styles, having been more influenced by the European modernism he saw, and when he did incorporate regional overtones, with the exception of the Plains Indians on the Clovis hotel, his buildings were restrained and simple. He favored aluminum and cast-concrete detailing on brick structures.

The entrance to the Curry County Courthouse is apparent but integrated into the overall massing and shallow setbacks. It is flanked by grooved piers and lower wings and is stepped at the parapet. The third story is delineated by a shallow setback and smaller piers. The Zia sun symbol is cast in concrete above the entrance. Merrell used New Mexico's heraldic device in another courthouse he designed during this decade, the Roosevelt County Courthouse, where the Zia sun is cast in aluminum spandrels. The sun motif had been selected by the state because all of the Pueblos recognize a sun diety, Pohe-yemo.

Spandrels of cast concrete on the Curry County Courthouse repeat this motif. Terracotta coping on the wings is composed of frets and chevrons, both of which could have been derived from Anasazi pottery, with its black-painted geometrics on white. Aluminum grilles over the ground-level doors repeat the sun motif, this time in the form of angular rays.

The Curry County Courthouse in Clovis, New Mexico, employs the New Mexico state symbol — the Zia Indian sun motif — on its entrance and spandrels.

Burgeoning populations clustered sporadically in the Southwest, and wide expanses of space separated them. Gentle hills and lush grazing land fill the hundreds of miles between Raton and Amarillo. Even if an architect worked out of a fairly large city, he or she still had to cover a vast geographical area to obtain the business essential for survival. W. C. Townes was one of those architects. Based in Amarillo, with a partner in Albuquerque, Raby Funk, he covered eastern New Mexico and western Texas. If an architect couldn't afford the travel time to supervise the construction phase, a local architect licensed by the state would do so—in this case, R. W. Voorhees.

Townes specialized in courthouses, designing a total of twenty-seven, including those of Quay County in New Mexico and Potter County in Texas. Expansion of the Santa Fe Railroad into Raton brought sufficient growth to warrant a new courthouse, replacing its 1897 Romanesque predecessor. The town applied for PWA funding to hire the most obvious choice, an architect specializing in courthouse design, and built the new courthouse.

The site of this courthouse slopes and overlooks the central business district. The structure itself has been assessed by architectural historian Marcus Whiffen as one of the two best Art Deco courthouses in the Southwest. He describes its massing:

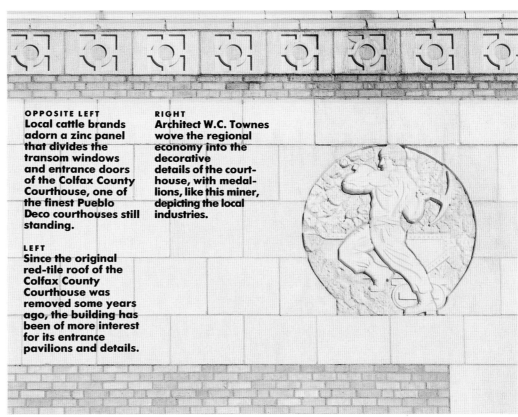

OPPOSITE LEFT
Local cattle brands adorn a zinc panel that divides the transom windows and entrance doors of the Colfax County Courthouse, one of the finest Pueblo Deco courthouses still standing.

LEFT
Since the original red-tile roof of the Colfax County Courthouse was removed some years ago, the building has been of more interest for its entrance pavilions and details.

RIGHT
Architect W.C. Townes wove the regional economy into the decorative details of the courthouse, with medallions, like this miner, depicting the local industries.

Its five part facade, brick and terra cotta, steps up from three-story wings to a five-story center, from which a three part entrance pavilion projects. By advancing each section of the facade and of the entrance pavilion slightly in front of its outer neighbor—with the result that there are five different wall planes—the structure has been given a dynamic centripetal movement horizontally as well as vertically, while the sense of the mass has been enhanced at the same time.(23)

Terra-cotta coping is cast with a simplified Zia sun motif dripping down the corners to form a stepped motif contrasting with the negative shape in buff brick. The pavilion is clad in terra-cotta and flanked by smallish rectangular panels decorated with steer heads. To reinforce the ranching economy as a motif, three zinc panels decorated with different ranchers' brands appear over the doors.

Below the red-tiled hipped roof, in mezzo-relievo, are large medallions, one on each side. A shirtless miner wields a pick, in profile against an ore car. Facing him in the other medallion is a farmer using a scythe. Typical of the thirties, these figures are characterized by a greater degree of modeling and the use of perspective. This shift in aesthetic direction is attributable to the WPA social realism. The figures on the earlier Potter County Courthouse are much flatter and stylized, with no reference to perspective: perfect examples of twenties Art Deco.

The interior of the courthouse is mildly Pueblo Deco. Light fixtures are geometric, as are the tile wainscoting and terrazzo floors, and a Zia motif is inlaid on the floor of the lobby.

ALBUQUERQUE INDIAN HOSPITAL

(Public Health Service Indian Hospital), 801 Vassar Drive NE, Albuquerque, New Mexico, 1934

Originally built as a tuberculosis sanatorium, this hospital has a lobby decorated with stenciled designs and enhanced by the profile of an Indian in the linoleum tile floor. It is not the profile of an idealized or Plains Indian. Instead, it is specifically the profile of a Navajo man wearing a bandana headband. The use of such a specific image is symbolic of a shift in the Bureau of Indian Affairs's attitude under President Roosevelt.

Remarkable as a barometer of change, this was the first BIA building to deviate from a standard design. Hans Stamm, the Chief of the Architectural Group of the BIA in Washington, D.C., was directed to consider the region's built environment before designing the sanatorium. It is apparent from the resulting structure that he spent enough time in the Southwest to become imbued with prehistoric and historic Pueblo architecture.

A central entrance flanked by two wings leads into the lobby. Colored stripes on the floor lead to the lobby, converging at the Navajo's profile and diverging for the various wings. The wings are defined by corbeled arches of enameled plaster; the corners are protected by copper guards. The walls of the lobby are faced with variagated beige terra-cotta. Just below the blue ceiling, stenciled with mustard, red, and brown geometrical and cloud motifs, is a cornice or band composed of a running zigzag interspersed with arrow motifs. Grooved piers break up the horizontal walls. All of the doorways and reception and display windows are decorated with stepped keystones.

BELOW
The stenciled band surrounding the lobby ceiling of the Indian Hospital in Albuquerque is composed of stylized arrows and clouds.

The stenciled arrow motifs and arrowheads are similar to those found on Navajo rugs woven in the Tec Nos Pas region. Regional rugs emerged during the 1920s when various traders with the Navajo Nation supervised the quality and even suggested modifications to the design and production of textiles to make them more appealing or saleable. J. B. Moore set an example in the Crystal region, suggesting the return to vegetal dyes, such as mistletoe, which produces a soft mustard, and indigo, which produces numerous shades of blues. The natural blacks, grays, and browns were used without over-dying to deepen their colors.

Only a few of Stamm's design elements are curvilinear; the rest, especially the diamonds on the ceiling and the arrow motifs, can be traced either to Two Grey Hills or Tec Nos Pas textiles. He apparently took the time to drive to the Four Corners area, west of Shiprock, perhaps in the spring when winds whip the mesas, tossing tumbleweeds into the air. There's a vaguely melancholy feeling then, a ghost-town sense of aimlessness.

Stamm also captured the Navajo's cultural debt to the Pueblo cultures on the exterior. During and after the Pueblo Revolt, the various nations became more interdependent. The Navajos adopted weaving and became seminomadic, even developing some agriculture. A T-shaped structure, the hospital is terraced in shallow tiers and steps. The original entrance is now concealed by an addition. The turquoise-green terra-cotta coping is fluted, the color a reference to Pueblo color symbolism and signifying divine fertility. An elongated terrace is created by two symmetrical stories rising to a third. Piers punctuate this level and are repeated again at the fourth story. The parapet is stepped in a cloud motif. The fifth-story setback has a stepped roofline. A tall chimney, used when the hospital was a sanatorium, appears behind the penthouse, a pinnacle to the overall pyramidal form.

The profile of a Navajo on the hospital's lobby floor is a specific reference to the patrons of this Bureau of Indian Affairs structure.

The stepped-cloud motif adorns both the exterior and interior of the Indian Hospital.

FEDERAL BUILDING

421 Gold Avenue, SW, Albuquerque, New Mexico

To be lifted above the boundaries of earth and gravity is surely magical. For our heavy bodies, flight seems to be a feat beyond imagination, and birds have justly been the messengers between the skies above and the earth below in shamanistic cultures, including those of the Native American. Inhabiting both worlds, birds are associated with transformation. Transgressing the limits of humans, they seem to be special messengers for prayers.

One bird, probably the eagle, was transformed by legend into the Great Thunderbird, an image found throughout the Plains Indian cultures, as well as those of the Southeast. The thunderbird combines the characteristics of the nomadic hunting society, which is more closely tied to warfare, and those of the peaceful maize farmers. This duality can be reduced simply to war and nurturing, and in the cosmic sense, death and rebirth. The appearance of an image of the thunderbird during a shamanistic vision quest practiced by Plains Indians warriors is interpreted by inverted behavior afterwards. A warrior who has seen the thunderbird laughs at the sacred, clowns about during serious rituals, behaving in the opposite way one would normally feel or react. "Great birds in the sky, wrapped in clouds," according to Indian legends, bring rain with the thunderheads, but also sow death, hurling thunderbolts; victims are struck by lightning. The thunderbird is a powerful mythological presence.

The architect of the Federal Building is undetermined; the cornerstone lists James B. Wetmore as supervising architect, but his role was purely administrative. The thunderbird is the building's leitmotif, appearing in five different variations. The American eagle is even interpreted as a thunderbird, flattened and stylized, each wing represented by a hooked triangle.

Three different colors of terra-cotta are used to emphasize different levels of the building. Cream-colored terra-cotta facing is relieved with bands of running thunderbirds, bearing a strong resemblance to those on the painted pottery at Hopi. Jesse Walter Fewkes excavated

The keystone in the entrance arch of the Federal Building in Albuquerque contains a terra-cotta thunderbird design.

ABOVE LEFT
Painted Hopi pottery may have been the source for the many varieties of birds used as details in the Federal Building.

ABOVE RIGHT
While the Hopi typically rounded the wings of their bird motifs, other Rio Grande Pueblos used more geometric and stylized imagery.

BELOW LEFT AND RIGHT
A variety of brick patterns enhances the terra-cotta cladding, bands, and relief tiles of the Federal Building's façades.

the prehistoric site of Sikyatki at Hopi and published the results of his research in 1919. He devoted a chapter to the bird imagery in his Bureau of American Ethnology publication. Food bowls and water vases were most frequently decorated with this imagery, often highly conventionalized.

The Federal Building reads like a short catalogue of bird variations. The running course at the first level is the most highly stylized image, with no figurative references. A stepped, terraced triangle is attached to a fret. Figures 311 and 350 of the Fewkes report contain elements the architect used in creating this band. Since the small squares diagonally opposed were unusual in pottery then being made, it's possible that the architect had read Fewkes.

The six-story building has a red-tiled, hipped roof surmounted by an octagonal cupola with a gilded lantern. The symmetry of the form is emphasized by a large arched entrance, reaching to the second story. The entrance is embellished with ochre terra-cotta facing. Vertical bands composed of zigzags and frets, intersected by crosses and sun motifs, outline the arch. The Navajo directional symbol appears in this band.

Motifs originating from the Hispanic culture, more curvilinear and floral, are used in the brass molding around the doors. Wrought-iron lamps on either side of the entry reinforce the introduction and assimilation of both Spanish and Mexican influences, also evident in the brackets below the roof. Terra-cotta faces only the first and second stories; the remainder is clad in variegated buff brick. Arched fenestration occurs below the roofline.

This building is a perfect realization of the cultures in the region: restrained yet innovative in the combination of the two forms within the public-building format. While it doesn't have the flamboyance of the KiMo Theater around the corner, it shouldn't, given its purpose. On the interior, a 1936 mural painted by Loren Mozley appears above the elevator doors. It illustrates the Pueblo Revolt.

ABOVE AND RIGHT
The Federal Building in Albuquerque fuses Hispanic, Hopi, and Navajo decorative devices. Its dramatic entrance is high- **lighted by a terra-cotta band with various Indian motifs, including the Navajo directional symbol and stylized birds.**

UNITED STATES POST OFFICE

201 South First Street, Gallup, New Mexico, 1933

It is strange that the town that has hosted the inter-Tribal Indian Ceremonial every August since the thirties, and is termed the "Gateway to Indian Country," does not have a post office that includes references to this important aspect of the town's economy. As early as 1776, the Navajo Nation had been mapped out by Father Anastasio Dominguez and Silvestre Escalante while exploring the region.

The Navajos, an Athabascan group, adopted Pueblo traits, including weaving, after the two cultures were thrown together following the Pueblo Revolt. By the eighteenth century, Spanish administrators were describing Navajo textiles as having more "delicacy and taste" than those woven by Hispanics. The Navajos' horsemanship and accumulation of horses, their large herds of sheep (the only animal capable of grazing on the spare mesas), and their tendency to raid the Pueblos and Hispanics gave them tremendous mobility, as well as a military freedom and a wealth not found among the Spanish-dominated Pueblos.

Gallup's economy was indebted to regional coal mining and to tourism brought in by Fred Harvey's El Navajo Hotel. Its commercial activity stemmed also from early trading posts in the region. S. Lorenzo Hubbell in Ganado, fifty-five

OPPOSITE
Wood volutes cap the concrete columns which support the entrance to the United States Post Office in Gallup, New Mexico.

miles away, founded a successful trading post in the late nineteenth century, following the example of Mormon traders. Blankets were traded for horses, and later for food and hard goods. C. N. Cotton, previously Hubbell's partner, moved to Gallup to become the first wholesaler in the area.

The railroad's arrival quickly increased the town's size. Navajos, who view jewelry as a form of currency, frequented the pawnshops which jostled each other on the streets. Movie theaters and a new county courthouse appeared. The town stretches along the railroad and then dribbles into red sandstone cliffs and the colored strata of the earth, for this is where

the Painted Desert becomes evident, with its mauves, grapes, grays, pale greens, and ochres.

A miniature bell tower on the southeast corner mitigates the axial symmetry of the entrance on South First Street. The red-tiled roof enhances the Hispanic references found on the bracketed portal. This one-story building is intimate in scale, seeming to embrace you as you walk up the steps to enter under the elaborate portal. Carved and painted in gay colors, it is supported by cast-concrete pillars decorated with wood corbels.

The combination of freestanding concrete pillars and wood brackets is an unusual note, especially when combined with other materials, including painted wood and brick. On either wing, flanking the portal, are cast-concrete cartouches. An eagle figure projects above the concrete coping. Mexican wrought-iron balconies inscribe the tall windows on each wing. The architects who worked under James B. Wetmore, Supervising Architect for the Treasury Department, are anonymous, since only his name appears on the cornerstone. Whoever was responsible for the design of this post office has integrated Art Deco and Hispanic regional influences in a pleasing way.

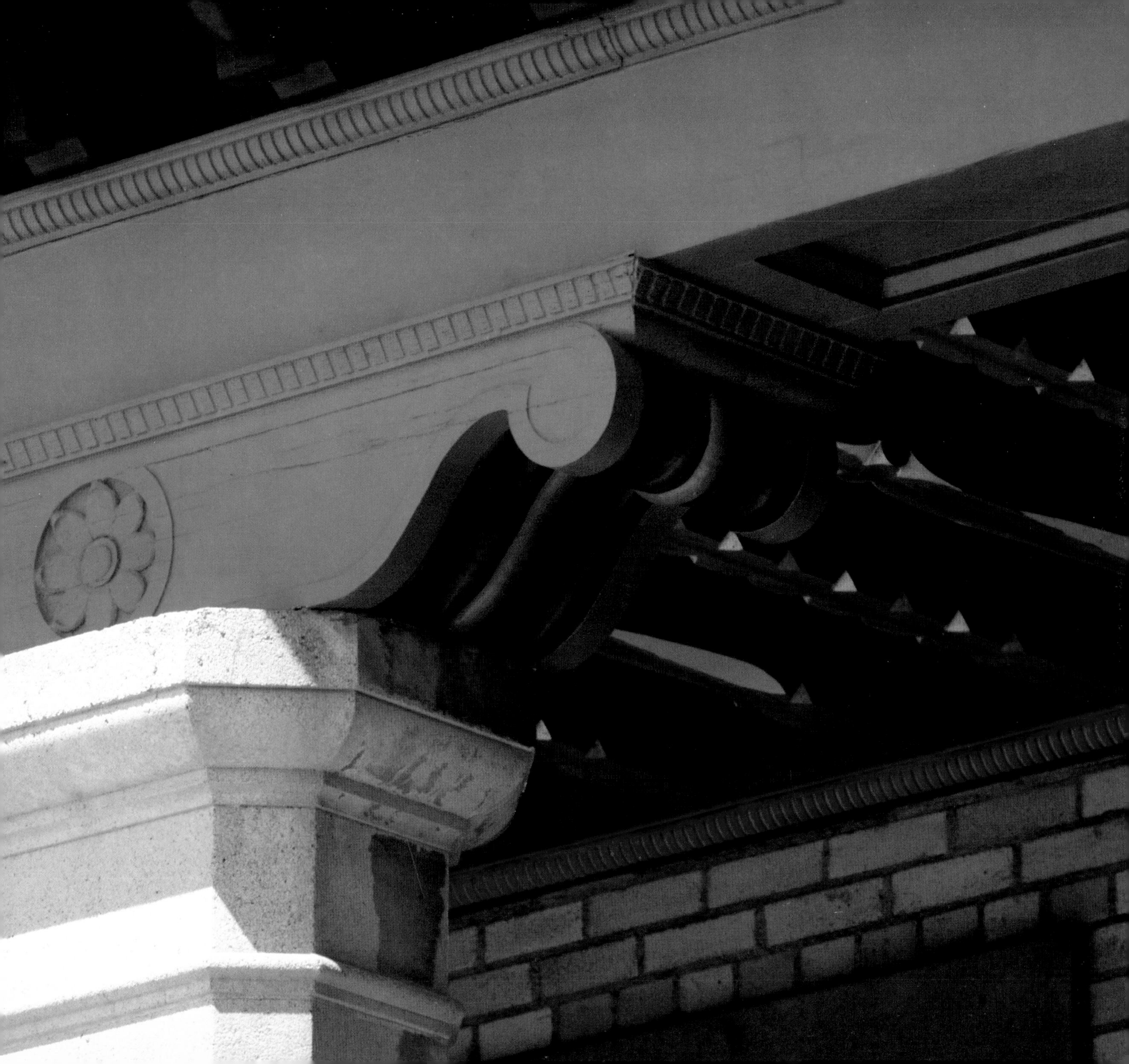

125 West Washington Street

Phoenix, Arizona, 1928

OPPOSITE
The City-County Building, an unusually massive and ornate example of the Pueblo Deco style, fills the west quadrant across from Patriot Square in downtown Phoenix.

Light fixtures at the Maricopa County entrance to the City-County Building take the form of arrows, with the feathers masking a cast-iron lamp.

t is not that unusual for a city and a county to share an office building. It is unusual, however, that one architect designed the building and the county's entrance, while another was engaged to distinguish the city's entrance. Edward Neild of Shreveport, Louisiana, was responsible for the overall scheme of this low, massive building with a red-tiled, hipped roof which encompasses the west side of Patriot Square.

The city entrance, facing west, was designed by the prominent Phoenix firm of Lescher and Mahoney. Leslie J. Mahoney had apprenticed in architectural firms in Los Angeles via an atelier that was affiliated with the Society of Beaux-Arts Architects in New York. Mahoney moved to Phoenix in 1912 to replace Royal W. Lescher's designer, who found Phoenix too hot! Lescher was not responsible for any design work, handling instead the commercial aspects of the practice.

Mahoney had to retain Neild's exterior elevation, while integrating the city's entrance. The portal is flanked by two huge phoenixes, geometrically modeled with strong planes. The brass doors are formed from six large panels, each containing a raised rosette. The hanging light fixture is especially ornamental and visibly influenced by Spanish decoration. Because of California's proximity, much of the Pueblo Deco

in Arizona leans more toward the Hispanic heritage than the Indian.

Neild's entrance is wider and faces north. Flanked by curved brackets with terra-cotta rosettes, the cast-iron light fixtures on each side are in the form of arrows. The points are formed from stylized thunderbirds and the feathers are, in actuality, the lamps, and consequently three-dimensional. This is an innovative variation and use of motifs.

This six-story structure (including a basement level with aboveground fenestration) is rusticated cast concrete at the first two floors, and is separated from the terra-cotta cladding of the upper stories by a stringcourse of running zigzags. Four-story wings flank the central portion and are further differentiated by balconies at the third story.

Terra-cotta details abound. All of the windows are separated by green-and-white spindles and finials that have the appearance of corn stalks. This imagery is continued in a foliated pattern framing the windows. Headers carry incised zigzags. Lattices cover the windows at the sixth floor. The parapet is decorated with curved brackets and rosettes.

The City-County Building is a complex and successful mass, conveying a seriousness of purpose and a relationship to the region.

LEFT
On the County
entrance to the City-
County Building the
flowery and curvi-
linear forms of
the bronze transom
grille are juxtaposed
with the heavily
grooved granite and
herringbone details
of the arch.

OPPOSITE
Scrolled brackets elegantly cap the piers lining the walls of the City-County Building.

RIGHT
The City entrance to the City-County Building is dramatically framed by two sculpted phoenixes, the mythical namesake of the city.

PHOENIX CITY HALL

NO TRESPASS

COCHISE COUNTY COURTHOUSE

Quality Hill, Bisbee, Arizona, 1931

As the Comanches were moved out of Texas and onto reservations in Indian Territory, now Oklahoma, they became increasingly disaffected with the promises made by Anglos and government agents. Food was scarce and the reservations were never large enough to sustain the traditional life-style by hunting. Buffalo herds were decimated by hunters shooting from trains, and other animals were increasingly scarce. The Comanches fought back desperately.

The Apaches, on the other hand, felt less threatened by the Anglos, since both had fought against the Mexicans. Shortly after the Gadsden Purchase in 1853, the pressure of cattle ranchers and miners began to be felt, even by the more amiable Apaches. Cochise was chief of the Chiricahua Apaches who inhabited the southeastern corner of present-day Arizona. His father-in-law, Mangas Coloradas (Red Sleeves), was chief of the Mimbreños of southern New Mexico. Together, they continued to resist, but they were ultimately unsuccessful against the rapid-fire military weapons and unsavory tactics of the army and other Indian scouts.

Cochise County comprises the area where Chief Cochise once roamed. After gold nuggets were found on a mesa near Wickenburg in 1863, the gold rush spread over Arizona. Tombstone, north of Bisbee, was at the center of the silver-mining industry, and Bisbee became the center of copper mining. The Lavender Queen Copper Mine, opened by Phelps Dodge Corporation, became the first big producer by the late 1880s.

Bisbee grew rapidly, initially attracting commercial activity as a result of its notorious Whisky Row.

Roy Place designed this courthouse to replace an earlier one, and the dedication of the new courthouse was celebrated in conjunction with Bisbee's fiftieth anniversary. Cast-concrete sculptures were designed by the architect's son and eventual successor, Lew Place, who was only seventeen at the time. These figures—grizzled miners panning and mining precious metals—form a stylized pediment in conjunction with the more traditional form below, which is decorated with two types of cactus: barrel and prickly-pear.

Bronze grilles over the doors depict Blind Justice surrounded by radiating rays. Angular lampposts and fixtures flank the entrance which marks the central, five-story bay. The upper floors house the jail. The wings flank this center portion at the fourth and second stories. The parapet along the entire façade is decorated with stepped piers and caps and at the upper stories with chevrons and schematized cactus. Built against the hill, the rear entrance is reached by a concrete walkway decorated with incised zigzags.

In architectural historian Marcus Whiffen's estimation, the courthouse is a masterpiece of Pueblo Deco, and Roy Place achieved "a more sculptural plasticity than most Art Deco ornament . . ."(24) The Cochise County Courthouse stands as an enduring tribute to the surrounding desert and the region's heritage.

The brass entrance doors to the Cochise County Courthouse in Bisbee, Arizona, display the twin figures of justice against a background of sun rays.

The sculpted miners above the courthouse's entrance pediment were designed by the architect's son, Lew Place, and represent the importance of mining to Bisbee's economy.

Stylized cactus motifs serve as spandrel and parapet details throughout the Cochise County Courthouse.

FIVE

COMMERCIAL BUILDINGS

The Xerox Building in Amarillo was originally designed as a theater with adjoining retail space.

Tons and tons of terra-cotta—to be precise, two thousand tons of the material—went on the New York Central Building in 1928. Flaunted by an industry publication, *Atlantic Terra Cotta*, this tremendous building features massive buffalo heads. The majority of commercial buildings erected in the twenties and thirties utilized terra-cotta as the primary means of ornament. Terra-cotta could be used to clad an exterior, to make decorative cornices and spandrels, and to cover interior walls and floors; even chimneys were manufactured from this versatile material. It was fireproof, easy to maintain, and most of all, relatively inexpensive to use. The age of industrialization had adapted to ornament. The architect could use this fired and glazed clay to replicate classical orders, Art Deco zigzags, or Gothic arches.

The material came into prominence with the modernistic impetus. Rather than relying on previous styles, the architect could design his own patterns, and the cost per unit would drop in proportion to duplication. (In fact, this was the theme of *Atlantic Terra Cotta* throughout the twenties.) Terra-cotta could be molded or incised with decorative elements. The colors were unlimited.

The February 1928 issue of *Atlantic Terra Cotta* featured small commercial buildings. The advantages of the material were pointed out as particularly desirable for the two- or three-story building, since it could provide "a front above the ordinary chaos of weather beaten and discolored building materials."(25) Color could be inexpensively introduced. Restaurants, theaters, and other buildings for amusement allowed the architect to experiment with fanciful decoration. An innovative facade on a commercial building acted to attract the consumer's attention, and was a form of advertising.

Some of the most outstanding commercial design was undertaken by the architect for the Samuel H. Kress Company, Edward F. Sibbert. Kress had developed strategies to lower the cost of department store items by stocking huge quantities of those items on the premises. He provided lunchrooms for shoppers and introduced brighter interior lighting than was ordinarily used, in order to stimulate sales.

Terra-cotta also played a role in the transition of modernism in the United States. An industry publication entered the fray of modernism versus modernistic (now considered to be Art Deco):

American architecture is in a state of transition with two clearly defined tendencies, similar in the use of color but diametrically opposed in form.

The tremendous scale of modern office, hotel, and apartment buildings creates a new problem.

In one case modeled ornament is giving way to colors: color on broad, flat surfaces, combined with skillful distribution of mass.

In another school, intricate modeled detail of "modern art" is applied on the plane of the building, the lines engraved instead of raised, the colors brilliant and varied. (26)

Until the depression affected construction costs, terra-cotta was the primary means of external decoration of commercial buildings. If you look at catalogues from the period, it is evident that the foliated patterns we associate with the French Exposition were stock patterns. But for the most part, the work in this medium was highly original and designed for each building.

Terra-cotta was gradually replaced in the thirties by cast and colored concrete, which never wore as well, could never be as brightly polychromed, and at best was only a second-rate material in comparison.

SOUTHWESTERN BELL TELEPHONE (MARKET EXCHANGE)

**2401 Chestnut Street,
Fort Worth, Texas, 1931**

New technologies and marketing concepts encouraged the use of a contemporary style. In the twenties, Bell Telephone Company embarked on a building program that embraced a style as modern as its communication system. Buildings constructed during this period were consciously Art Deco. The company's buildings in the Southwest were no exception. One fabulous example remains intact in Fort Worth—the Market Exchange. Southwestern Bell's architect was Irving Ray Timlin, who designed the majority of the company's buildings in the Dallas-Fort Worth region in the late twenties and early thirties.

The Market Exchange was created by Timlin to mesh unobtrusively with a residential neighborhood. Clad in buff brick, the two-story building is copiously ornamented with terra-cotta of the same color. The terra-cotta coping is interrupted with a stepped parapet and occasionally with a sun motif. The stepped lintels are inscribed with a highly stylized and not-quite-historical image of downtown Fort Worth: Nineteenth-century buildings are interspersed with modern ones as the street recedes into the sun; billowing clouds hover over the skyline.

The other dominant motif is the zigzag, which runs horizontally across some window lintels and vertically around the door jamb in stylized jamb shafts. Except for the recessed entrance and ground-level windows, the building is very planar, its form a rectangle.

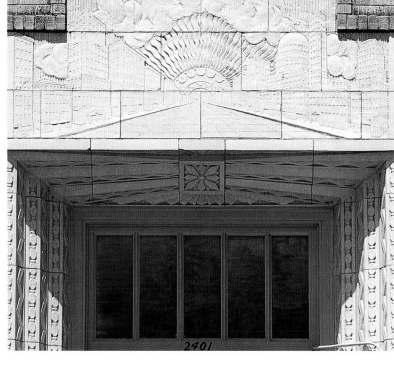

A terra-cotta lintel on the Southwestern Bell Telephone Market Exchange Building displays an image of an idealized, twentieth-century Fort Worth skyline.

Southwestern Bell, like many other companies in the Southwest, adopted the Pueblo Deco style as a corporate vernacular.

S.H. KRESS

1107 Broadway,
Lubbock, Texas, c. 1934

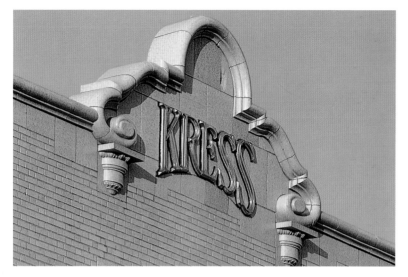

I f you came into Lubbock to shop at Kress, you knew you were in the heart of cattle country, even if you didn't know it by riding fence in the spring or cleaning out water holes. Edward F. Sibbert found his job with Samuel H. Kress through the want ads in the *New York Times*, and it was a partnership of the type that arises purely by chance. Sibbert was an innovative architect. He had the imagination to manipulate the vocabularies of modernism and Art Deco to create a corporate style that offered variation within the economic and commercial strictures devised by Kress.

This Kress store is a three-story brick building faced with butterscotch-colored terra-cotta. The parapet is elegantly scalloped, vaguely referential to that architectural symbol of Texas, the Alamo. In San Antonio, near the original Alamo, Sibbert created an S. H. Kress that is a direct rephrasing of the original. His Lubbock store ingeniously employs large-scale scallops on the parapet and the scallop motif over the fenestration and cornercaps.

Sibbert had fun with the ranching motif, creating tie-rod brackets in the geometricized form of Hereford cattle. A canopy extends the length of the façade and is made from incised bronze. Black marble runs along the base of the building. The display windows are rounded, as Streamline concepts began to enter Sibbert's vocabulary. This building has some similarities to the Kress store in Amarillo—the bronze canopy and the black marble base below the display windows—but the Lubbock store has a more distinct personality.

The tie-rod brackets on the exterior of this Kress store are in the shape of a Hereford steer, reflecting Lubbock's primary industry.

Edward Sibbert, architect for the Lubbock Kress, was responsible for designing over 200 stores throughout the twenties, thirties, and forties — each store reflective of the local crafts and customs.

WHITE & KIRK BUILDING

516 South Polk Street, Amarillo, Texas, 1938

TOP
The prototype for this yucca frieze on the White & Kirk Department Store in Amarillo was carved on a bar of Ivory soap.

ABOVE
The White & Kirk Department Store in Amarillo was designed by Guy Carlander.

Guy A. Carlander worked for the Atchison Topeka & Santa Fe Railroad in Chicago while he studied at the Chicago Art Institute. The architectural division of the railroad had been strongly influenced by Charles Whittlesey, innovator of the line's successful Spanish Pueblo look in the West. This influence was apparent in Carlander's early work. He launched his private practice in Amarillo in 1920, riding the crest of oil discoveries two years earlier. Carlander was busy during the twenties, designing schools, a local hospital, and several hospitals for the Santa Fe in other cities of the West. He continued to modify his style until it became uniquely his: Pueblo Streamline with moderate use of decoration.

The Texas Panhandle is space, more space, mesquite, lazy clouds, cattle, and clusters of oil wells. The Fort Worth & Denver City Railroad preceded the town of Amarillo, which grew at a juncture where the line curves around Amarillo Lake. The first wooden buildings here were painted *amarillo*, the Spanish word for yellow. Intentionally or not, much of the brick produced in this region during the first third of the twentieth century was a yellow buff.

How many terra-cotta motifs have been carved in an Ivory Soap bar? Carlander's wife recounted how her husband, after making drawings of the yucca cactus, which forms a band above the first floor of the White & Kirk building, then carved it in soap. The angle formed by the long spines of this cactus are joined in a more typical Deco touch: a ninety-degree angle of concentric circles. The vertical bands of windows rise to stepped pyramids (since destroyed in a rehabilitation for office space). A steel-framed structure, this four-story department store is faced with buff brick. The terra-cotta has a beige glaze. The simple rectangular form is offset by the circulation tower and stepped pylons.

Carlander designed other notable work during the thirties, such as Ordway Hall at Amarillo Junior College and the gymnasium at the same campus, but the White & Kirk was to be his only work in the Pueblo Deco style. The elegance of the flowering-yucca motif leaves a lasting impression and a reminder that he often successfully integrated textures, ornament, and context.

THE XEROX BUILDING

(Originally the Paramount Theater)

817 South Polk Street, Amarillo, Texas, 1932

The Xerox building was originally designed as a theater with adjacent office space. The tall entrance pavilion was enhanced by a vertical marquee, which was removed during remodeling. W. Scott Dunne's building still has a wonderful feeling around the parapet. Like almost every commercial building in Amarillo from this period, it is of yellow brick. The parapet and coping are terra-cotta. Red, green, and white polychrome floral motifs decorate the piers, which rise above the zigzagged parapet, as well as the taller entrance pavilion. Grooved piers are footed with black marble. Dunne, a noted Dallas architect, created a theater that reflected the wealth engendered by oil wells.

The parapet of the Xerox Building in Amarillo is formed from a zigzag coping, punctured by piers with floral motifs in red, white, and green—a rare color combination.

S. H. KRESS

700 South Polk Street, Amarillo, Texas, 1932

Edward Sibbert's three-story building is finished at the raised parapet with crenellated coping in stepped-back layers. Like many commercial buildings in the early years on the Western frontier, it has a false front. The decorative interest of this simple building is primarily found in patterned brickwork surrounding the fenestration and tie-rod brackets. Another band of patterned brickwork occurs at the level of the third-story lintels. The terra-cotta lintels are the same color as the buff brick, with a zigzag motif.

As other architectural historians have noted (in reference to his New York, S. H. Kress building), Sibbert often injected terra-cotta details that referred to items sold in the store—in this case, potted plants. If you look carefully at the drawing of the Polk Street elevation details, you will see that Sibbert apparently changed his mind after drawing the polychrome floral detail, inserting a flowerpot on the building instead. The canopy is more intricately designed than the one over the Lubbock store. A circulation tower appears at the rear of the store, and bears a resemblance to Carlander's tower on the White & Kirk Building.

While Sibbert was with Kress, he often used gold-enameled terra-cotta letters—just the use suggested by the Atlantic Terra Cotta Company. In fact, Sibbert's work so often utilized terracotta that one of his buildings appeared on the cover of a 1930s Federal Seaboard Terra Cotta Company brochure. Metallic gold terra-cotta was termed "Noble metal finish," and was created via a technique involving the melting of metals onto the tiles in a second, high-temperature firing.

ABOVE
Spanish for yellow, Amarillo produced a buff-colored brick used in many city structures, including this S.H. Kress Department Store.

RIGHT
Although the Kress store in Amarillo was not as elaborate as others in Texas, the architect, Edward Sibbert, made imaginative use of brick patterns and terra-cotta.

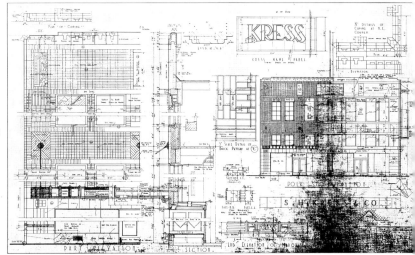

SKINNER BUILDING

8th Street and Central Avenue SW, Albuquerque, New Mexico, 1931

Located near the Country Club district, this has to be the most fabulous grocery store in the Southwest. The architect, A. W. Boehning moved to the "Land of Enchantment" to treat his tuberculosis, as did at least two other architects of this era, John Gaw Meem and Carlos Vierra. Boehning began his career apprenticing in the Trost and Trost firm, and in 1924 he opened up a practice of his own. He was interested in the regional arts, collecting pottery and blankets, and had an extensive library of books on the various topics related to this interest. The grocery store is one of the few buildings he designed that is overtly Pueblo Deco; he generally leaned toward Mission and Spanish Colonial styles.

The building is clad in a pale, shimmering, white terra-cotta decorated with various motifs. The cornice contains an imbrication motif, repeated with a variation above the opalescent glass transom windows that run across the façade and the west elevation. Stepped diamonds form a band of white against the green background of these transoms. A bronze-covered transom bar is termed in Boehning's elevation as having "modernistic design." Piers, fluted of course, mark the corners and occur along the west side. Ventilation grilles appear below display windows. Pier caps are treated like terminus figures, disappearing into the plane of the pier.

ABOVE
The Skinner Building in Albuquerque is a rare example of the Pueblo Deco style—a grocery store.

LEFT
The volutes on the terra-cotta piers of the Skinner store make subtle use of Navajo and Pueblo motifs.

RIGHT
The S.H. Kress Department Store in El Paso is covered with ornate terra-cotta from cladding to finials.

INSET
The *mirador* on this Kress store conceals mechanical equipment, and was given an elaborate pinnacle to disguise its presence.

94

Oregon and Mills Streets, El Paso, Texas, 1937

El Paso is a gateway to Mexico. Across the Rio Grande sprawls Mexico's second largest city, Juárez. Often the two cities are almost indistinguishable; pastel stucco houses dot the hillsides, interspersed with cacti. The soft cadences of Spanish surround you on the streets. Go into the Kress store and hear salsa and *rancheria* music playing overhead. Located in the central business district near the bridge crossing into Juárez, the store stands out as a lavish tribute to Spanish architecture as only Edward F. Sibbert could design.

The architect for the Samuel H. Kress Company from 1929 until 1954, Sibbert was a commanding designer who could elegantly improvise within the strictures of the formula for a retail store. Of the 200-plus stores he designed during his tenure, more than thirty are either on the National Register of Historic Places or in designated Historic Districts. The El Paso Kress Store is distinguished by being one of Sibbert's two favorite designs, the other being the flagship store on Fifth Avenue in New York, which has since been destroyed.

Built in an **L** shape on the block between Oregon Street on the west and Mesa Avenue on the east, it faces Mills Street, except where a chunk is bitten out on the corner of Mesa and Mills. All of the elevations are faced with a light beige terra-cotta supplied by the Gladding & McBean Company in California for Kress buildings west of the Mississippi. Sibbert often had to supply models for the molds as he rarely utilized stock elements.

The Mesa Avenue elevation rises four stories, divided by three piers capped at the parapet with fanciful finials with brackets of red, gold, and turquoise. Flanking either side are lunette-headed windows with wrought-iron balconies. Sibbert played with the lunette header as a motif here, and it is repeated as a sort of cornice in polychrome terra-cotta. Because of the false balconies with wrought-iron grilles, you almost

Inspired primarily by Spanish and Mexican architecture, the El Paso Kress store contains a single Indian reference—a wrought-iron railing in the form of a cumulus cloud.

feel as if you're in an atmospheric theater in Tampa, Florida.

The Oregon Street elevation is not entirely devoid of windows, but it does have very few above the ground floor. A 1935 article in *Architectural Forum* about Sibbert's New York Kress store explains how the design conforms to a marketing strategy:

Essentially it is a department store, carrying over 3,500 items in stock. Unlike the average department store, it devotes its entire selling area to selling, with its storage space concentrated in a warehouse that occupies the bulk of the upper floors. So rapid is the turnover that the warehouse must be on the premises... (27)

This explains why Sibbert's buildings often had so few windows on the upper levels and probably why he incorporated decorative devices such as false windows and balconies. The El Paso Kress has small false windows at the ground level on Oregon Street.

The tower gives the building a tremendous presence. It resembles a *mirador*—a concealed or latticed space where Islamic women could see but not be seen. In reality it conceals the mechanical operations for air conditioning and elevators. Other details on the Kress store reveal Sibbert's awareness of the Alhambra in Spain. He has transformed decorative elements from the latter, especially the rosette motifs, streamlining and simplifying them here. The lattice covering the tower resembles those on balconies at the Alhambra. A Spanish rope motif surrounds the windows. Brackets are placed above the windows where a keystone would be if the windows were arched.

Kress scholar Bernice Thomas notes that Sibbert always strove to make his buildings stand out, but not too much. The El Paso Kress must be the exception: It is one of his most flamboyant creations and would stand out in any context.

LEFT
Numerous details on the El Paso Kress were derived from the Alhambra in Spain.

OPPOSITE RIGHT
The lunette headers on the Kress windows have a "diaper" of terra-cotta.

OPPOSITE FAR RIGHT
Architect Edward Sibbert was adept at manipulating traditional architectural vocabularies for his own purposes. Here, a keystone is transformed into a spandrel element.

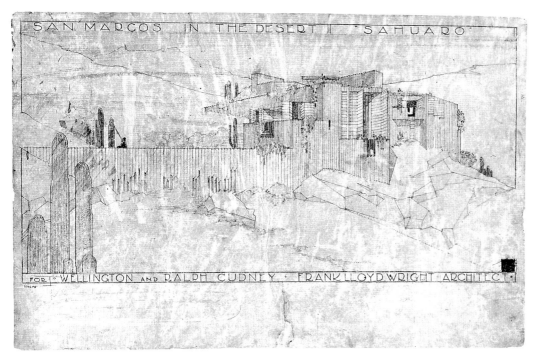

SAN MARCOS IN THE DESERT "SAHUARO"

FOR WELLINGTON AND RALPH CUDNEY · FRANK LLOYD WRIGHT ARCHITECT

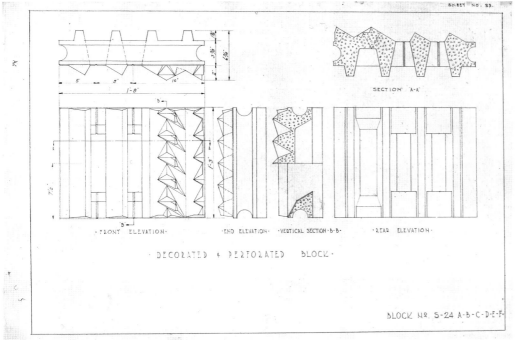

SHEET NO. 23.

SECTION 'A-A'

· FRONT ELEVATION ·   · END ELEVATION · · VERTICAL SECTION· B·B·   · REAR ELEVATION ·

· DECORATED & PERFORATED BLOCK ·

BLOCK NO. S-24 A-B-C-D-E-F.

TALIESIN WEST

Maricopa Mesa, Scottsdale, Arizona, 1938

LEFT
Frank Lloyd Wright designed a modified textile block for the Wellington and Ralph Cudney residence at San Marcos-in-the-Desert.

BOTTOM LEFT
The modified concrete block, with its fluted zigzags, takes as its source the saguaro cactus.

The metropolitan area of Phoenix was first settled by farmers and developers who perceived that a city could once again rise from the flames of the desert by relying on prehistoric Hohokam Indian irrigation canals for water. Remnants of these canals could still be seen in the nineteenth century, and by the 1890s a series of large and small canals fed fields of cotton, tobacco, citrus, and other crops.

The invitation to work with his former student, Warren McArthur, Jr., must have seemed propitious to Frank Lloyd Wright, coming as it did during a period of personal problems. The sunlight and openness of the Southwest shimmered like a mirage before him. Engaged to advise McArthur regarding the use of the textile block, Wright quickly gained a commission from an individual, Dr. Alexander Chandler, interested in building a large desert resort. Originally planned for the town of Chandler, south of Phoenix, the San Marcos-in-the-Desert Project was never realized. For the resort project, Wright adapted the saguaro cactus as a motif for his textile blocks. The stylization of this motif perfectly reflected the desert ambience.

The hotel was to have been accompanied by several houses (also unbuilt). The resort was designed to include a central lobby, dining room,

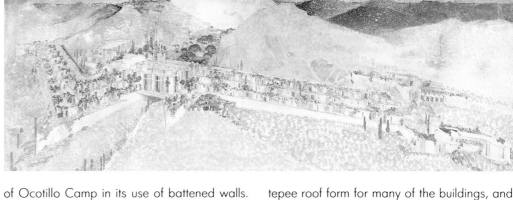

and wings to accommodate the guest rooms. During the several years Wright worked on the drawings for this project, he camped out in what became a prototype for Taliesin West. Wright constructed this temporary atelier, Ocotillo Camp, from lightweight wood and canvas. The camp structures sufficed until he was able to build his permanent home and office at Taliesin West. All of his drawings from this period used a stepped motif, and it is apparent in this desert context that Wright derived the motif from the Pueblo Indians rather than from the Mayans, whose architecture inspired his California textile-block houses built a decade earlier.

The form of Taliesin West resembled that of Ocotillo Camp in its use of battened walls. Built of more durable materials, rough, pebble-ladden cast-concrete and wood, the permanent atelier allowed him to explore the ideas tentatively suggested at Ocotillo Camp. The truncated pyramid appears as a motif, both in the forms of the buildings and for doorways and windows. Exaggerated overhangs provide cool shadows. Deep apertures, recessed doorways, and small windows with shutters contribute to shade. The effect of the cast-concrete is softened by the use of wood.

Wright was interested in the Indians, those in Wisconsin and those in the Southwest. The 1924 drawings for the Nakota Country Club used a tepee roof form for many of the buildings, and large-scale Indians (a chief and his squaw) were to have flanked the entrance.

Wright was one of the most influential architects of his time, and all of his projects received tremendous attention from the general public and professionals alike. His textile houses and the Tokyo Imperial Hotel created ripples of influence for years and had a great impact on the adoption of Art Deco in the United States. If any of his skyscrapers had been built during the twenties (he designed various projects), his impact would have been even greater in the realm of commercial architecture.

LUHRS TOWER

45 West Jefferson Street, Phoenix, Arizona, 1930

Stucco, a material resembling adobe, effectively clads the Luhrs Tower in Phoenix—the only Pueblo Deco skyscraper.

**OPPOSITE
Conquistadores ornament the upper stories of the Luhrs Tower.**

Camelback Mountain kneels at the northern flank of Phoenix, an oasis surrounded by desert replete with saguaro and ocotilla cacti. Little shade is afforded by the paloverde, a tree without leaves. Apaches, Pimas, and Navajos once roamed here, but preceding them was a culture, the Hohokam (Pima word meaning "vanished"), that built pueblos sustained by irrigation. The Spanish and Mexican presence is visible here, too. The lush fields and groves of citrus fruit appeared after John Swilling noticed the pattern of the Hohokam canals and reinstituted a system fed by the Salt River from the mountains to the east in the 1860s. Phoenix rapidly became an agricultural center, supplying mining towns to the north with fresh produce.

The Spanish Colonial style seemed appropriate here, so low stucco buildings and red-tile roofs abounded. Even by the twenties, the concepts of modern architecture based on Chicago or European functionalism were not terribly evident, that is, until the advent of Art Deco. George Luhrs owned various properties surrounding Patriot Square, the heart of the business district in Phoenix. In 1928 a developer, Jerome H. Toy, wrote to him, "I believe there is an opening on your corner for a Law building, being so close to the new courthouse. I would suggest that all attorneys in Phoenix be lined up before they get located in the Security Building— I have a live man who could handle this angle of work successfully, if you care to make use of him." (28)

Paso. The firm's technical edge resulted in the commission of almost every tall building in the major cities of the region for twenty-five years. Trost had also developed several unique styles. He meshed Sullivanesque ornament with a modified Mission type of structure; the Owls Club in Tucson is a perfect example of his work in Arizona. In New Mexico, he built several wonderful and influential Pueblo Deco buildings, such as the Hotel Franciscan.

While working on the twelve-story Luhrs Tower, Trost was simultaneously designing and supervising the construction of Bassett Tower in El Paso, which was one story higher.

Completed in 1930, Luhrs Tower rises in two series of setbacks, at the ninth and twelfth floors. It is one of the few skyscrapers anywhere with a stucco exterior. Designer Paul Frankel wrote in the 1920s:

Rough plaster walls have come forward in the modern scheme of decoration and their great value lies in the surface texture that is produced. This texture often creates a harmonious character with many modern settings. It has one great and distinct advantage. It allows for an interplay of light and shadow and this is a characteristic of which we do not tire easily." (29)

Just below the red-tiled, hipped roof are green terra-cotta conquistadores, their armored torsos capping a pier, two on the east and two on the west elevations. Green plant motifs appear at the setbacks.

The first floor was devoted to retail space and has large display windows. Each window is headed by bands of two-dimensional floral motifs, combining Deco and Spanish aesthetics. The entrance is faced with granite, and various marbles are used as wainscoting on the entrance and lobby.

Luhrs Tower was never as influential as Trost's major Pueblo Deco hotel, the Franciscan, but the stucco exterior and amusing conquistadores do make it one of the outstanding skyscrapers of the period.

Henry C. Trost was that "live" man, chief architect of the firm Trost and Trost, located in El Paso, Texas. Specializing in reinforced-concrete structures since its inception in 1903, the firm was the largest and most important in the Southwest.

Trost had worked in Chicago before coming to the West in the late 1890s. He assimilated elements of the Chicago style and deftly conveyed a technical understanding of the underlying engineering in such buildings as Anson Mills in El

ECCLESIASTICAL BUILDINGS

The Church of the Most Precious Blood in Long Island City, New York, is one of the few Pueblo Deco churches in the United States.

By definition, religious buildings have a very specific purpose: the devotion to or celebration of God. The design of a temple, church, or mosque is strictly prescribed by the religion—its traditions and tenets. There are usually other buildings in addition to the place of worship: schools for religious instruction, halls for social activities, and rectories where the priests live. The one aspect all ecclesiastical buildings have in common is the perception of that place as a sacred space.

Roman Catholic churches have very specific areas related to different functions of the liturgy. The sanctuary is where priests perform their functions during the celebration of Mass. The choir is situated at the back of the church above the entrance and faces the sanctuary. The central portion, the nave, is the place where the congregation is assembled.

The sanctuary is usually elevated and divided by a railing at which Communion may be taken. The altar always has a figure of Christ on the cross. The early Spanish churches in the Southwest had figurative and highly decorated paintings of Christ and other saints on wooden panels, forming reredos behind the altar.

Cast concrete was used to build various churches in the first fifty years of the twentieth century, and it was easily adapted to the Art Deco aesthetic. The most fabulous Art Deco church, the Church of the Most Precious Blood in Long Island City, New York, was published in the magazine *Atlantic Terra Cotta*.

CHURCH OF THE MOST PRECIOUS BLOOD

32-23 36th Street, Long Island City, New York, 1932

The architect for this church, Henry J. McGill, retired from his architectural practice two years after finishing this project to become chief librarian at the Avery Library on the Columbia University campus. It is one of the most fabulous Art Deco churches in the United States and clearly derived from New Mexican Mission churches.

The interior is heavily clad in terra-cotta. A high wainscoting encircles the nave. Bands of interlocking diamonds alternate with plain bands in the wainscoting. Larger polychrome faience tiles are scattered about, and depict religious subjects, while others are floral or decorated with fleur-de-lis. The floor of the raised altar is covered with multicolored terra-cotta tiles. Marble was used to face the altar and altar walls. Cast-aluminum grilles are terraced.

The terraced motif appears in every facet, from the Stations of the Cross to the aluminum grilles covering lights, to the arches leading into supplementary chapels. *Atlantic Terra Cotta* magazine described it in these words: "...although one of the most modern in the country, [the church] still conforms to every liturgical requirement and its novel beauty will undoubtedly influence the ecclesiastical architecture of the future." (30) The issue was devoted to the adapta-

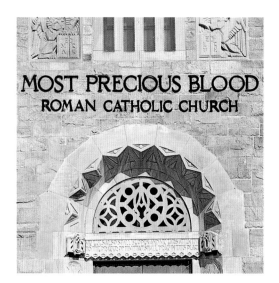

MOST PRECIOUS BLOOD
ROMAN CATHOLIC CHURCH

ABOVE
Cast concrete forms the transom grille, decorative panels, and the chevrons surrounding the arched entrance of the Church of the Most Precious Blood.

RIGHT
The rich terra-cotta wainscoting on the interior of the church mixes plain and diamond-patterned courses along with polychromatic tiles representing a variety of religions.

OPPOSITE
This crucifix, above the altar of the church, is an example of the stylization of figures during the Deco period.

tions of terra-cotta to ecclesiastical buildings and emphasized the idea that terra-cotta could appear in any style. It was the only Art Deco building included; the others were in the more popular Gothic and Renaissance Revival styles.

The exterior of the church is less overtly Pueblo Deco. It features a central nave with ten bays, an interesting steeple, and a smaller building to house the priest.

RESIDENTIAL BUILDINGS

At sunset, a Pueblo may appear a lambent gold, but could it really be mistaken for that precious metal? Visions of cities covered with gold compelled Spanish *conquistadores* to explore farther and farther north. By the time Coronado's expedition reached Taos Pueblo, it was surely discovered that the fabled "gold" was no more than the micaceous particles of adobe stucco. After the pyramids and the great wealth of the Aztecs and Mayans, the Pueblos encountered by the Spanish seemed meager and the landscape forlorn.

Pueblo Indians are the descendants of the Anasazi, a sophisticated prehistoric culture with trade routes extending to the Aztec Empire. Flourishing, the Anasazi built large urban centers, like the one at Chaco Canyon in New Mexico.

Pueblo Bonito, the largest housing complex at Chaco, was highly organized, indicating a conceptual frame of reference and specialized labor. Constructed of fine masonry and stuccoed with mud, this planned housing is not subordinated or incidental to the ritual spaces. Pueblo Bonito consisted of more than 800 apartments or rooms, among which were interspersed kivas—subterranean circular ceremonial spaces.

The kivas contained altars and paintings related to creation and fertility, both psychic and natural.

Because the Pueblos relied upon rainfall for agriculture, birds—and their relation to the sky where rain originates—had ritual significance. Motifs derived from birds and clouds predominated (and still do) among the Pueblo cultures. Irrigation sustained the agriculture to support a large population. An urban center, Chaco was surrounded by smaller communities linked by a network of roads.

Mysteriously, after building pueblos around plazas, now considered by architect Jerome Iowa to be dissident forms, opposed to the theocratic temple complexes of the Mesoamericans, the Anasazi abandoned Chaco, approximately 250 years before the arrival of the Spanish. Dispersing and scattering into smaller units, the Pueblos maintained a continuity of tradition and ritual.

Since there wasn't any gold, the Spanish assigned secondary importance to the region. Slowly, missions were established, and Hispanic settlement evolved. A Pueblo revolt in the seventeenth century drove the Spanish out for a short time but couldn't prevent their eventual return. Buildings at the pueblos were affected by the Spanish. Ladders through the roof and smoke holes were replaced by conventional doors, windows, and chimneys.

Mission churches rose, towering over secular structures. Time moved slowly until fur traders and other Anglos arrived. The United States began exploring and mapping the region in the first half of the nineteenth century. With territorial status came trains, and more rapid change. The agrarian-based economy expanded to include mining, forestry, and tourism.

Chaco was rediscovered. The Mindeleffs, archaeologists excavating Chaco, published their mapping and survey of the site in the Eighth Annual Report of the Bureau of American Ethnology in 1897. Other archaeologists were working at Hopi Pueblo and various sites in Arizona. Cliff dwellings at Mesa Verde in Colorado excited great interest in the Anasazi culture. The region gained a special significance because of the Native American cultures and architecture, coinciding with the ending of military efforts to eradicate tribes and nations.

The infatuation with Indians was manifested in the numerous magazine articles that appeared on the subject, a museum in New York devoted to George C. Heye's collections of Indian material, and Fred Harvey's use of the In-

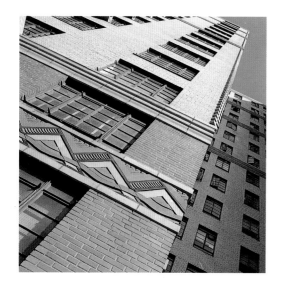

dian as image. Artists, too, contributed to this recognition. Joseph Sharp moved to Taos in the 1890s, and he often used men or women from the Pueblo as models. His use of dramatic lighting, and his perception of the inherent nobility and dignity of these people,popularized the culture. Still, society must have reeled when heiress Mable Dodge married Tony Lujan, an Indian from the Pueblo.

The seat of Spanish, Mexican, and finally territorial government, Santa Fe, is essentially rural. Meadow larks can be heard in the fields; sage wraps the town. The roads were still dirt into the twentieth century, and horse-drawn carts could still be seen. In the mountains to the east, villages fan out: Rosiata, situated among fields of wild iris, Truchas, nestled between small valleys, and Chimayo, at the end of a torturous road, have all been here since the Spanish. In Santa Fe, the dusty, winding, Camino del Monte Sol was home to various artists and writers who shared a passion for the West. The paintings and drawings of Gerald Cassidy, Maynard Dixon, and John Sloan reflected this passion. They and others worked with architects, archaeologists, and historians to preserve an ambience that carried the past into the present.

Because California had been settled by Americans during the gold rush, there was now greater awareness throughout the country of the Spanish Missions, such as the San Carlos de Borromeo in Carmel. The Mission style was seen as an appropriate expression for the West. The Louisiana Purchase Central Exposition, held in 1904 in St. Louis, popularized this style, and Mission bungalows began to appear in the Midwest. The 1907 Cos Cob Power Plant introduced red-tile roofs, scalloped gables, and beige stucco to Connecticut. After a few years, interest on the national level waned. Arizona and California were the exception; in these states the style enthusiastically continued.

A Pueblo style was being created during this period in New Mexico. Brown-stuccoed buildings with projecting vigas and asymmetrical massing began to appear on the University of New Mexico campus in Albuquerque. Other examples of, or interest in, the style were less evident at the turn of the century, however. Mary Jane Colter was one of the few architects working with Native American forms and motifs until another surge of interest occurred as the direct result of New Mexico's pavilion at the Panama-California Exposition of 1915 in San Diego.

The Gramercy House apartment complex in New York City employs a mix of Pueblo Deco and International Style decorative devices, such as these terra-cotta zigzag reliefs.

The Cliff Dweller might seem to be an enigmatic building, predating as it did much of the Pueblo Deco in the Southwest. Did Herman Lee Meader, the architect, travel by train, stay at Harvey Houses, and visit the cliff dwellings in Bandelier or Mesa Verde?

It is more likely that he attended the 1915 Panama-California Exposition at Balboa Park in San Diego. There, the New Mexico Pavilion was awarded first prize for originality and judged most popular by those attending the exposition. The pavilion housed an exhibition based on archaeological research at various sites. A display of a Pueblo "apartment complex fascinated urban dwellers who thought their own communal dwellings were uniquely modern," according to one news account. This was the second exposition to feature an exhibition of cliff dwellings; the 1904 Louisiana Purchase Central Exposition also featured the architecture of the Anasazi culture.

Isaac Hamilton Rapp had been selected by Edgar Lee Hewett and Sylvanus Morley, among others, to design the pavilion—New Mexico's first exposition entry after it became a state in 1912. The importance of this event made it imperative that the entry be unique and reflect a style known as *Pueblo* or *Santa Fe*. Rapp had few models to guide him, either in his own work or that of others. The only examples, other than the University of New Mexico campus, were to be found among either Mary Colter's work or at the Pueblos themselves. The pavilion indicates that Rapp was familiar with the Mission churches at Taos and Acoma.

The Pueblo style is characterized by softly rounded corners, deeply modeled recesses and apertures, often asymmetrical massing, a use of shadows, such as those created by vigas extending beyond a wall, and buttresses.

Meader's Cliff Dweller lacks Pueblo form or massing but compensates with its explicitly Indian motifs. Originally built as an apartment/hotel, the Cliff Dweller has an incredible awareness of its function as part of Riverside Drive both at the pedestrian level and in the streetscape as a whole. Situated on a corner that curves, the apartments can be seen from both the north and south. Friezes wrap around the corners of this wedge-shaped building.

Brick is patterned at the first-floor and basement levels, protruding in textured stepped diamonds. An incised concrete frieze ends at pendants before cornering the structure. Mountain lions stalk the frieze, which is stepped periodically and punctuated by masks, inspired either by kachinas or Mesoamerican masks. The tiny human skulls in some of the masks are a distinctly Mesoamerican trait. Buffalo heads, with ears of corn forming pendants, appear on the corner piers.

The entrance has been clumsily remodeled, but the lobby is still reasonably intact. Salt-glazed floor tiles in soft ochres and browns and wrought-iron grilles in a stepped diamond motif suggest that Meader was exposed to Navajo textiles, also displayed at the New Mexico Pavilion. Any stepped motif might be related to Rapp's design; a widely published photograph at the time, of an interior fireplace with a stepped opening, was made by Jesse Nusbaum. Decorative friezes and brickwork appear again on the upper levels of the Cliff Dweller.

This rare example of Pueblo Deco remains because it constitutes an entire building; interiors are more ephemeral but are known to have existed in New York City. The interior of Alfred C. Bossom's apartment was published in a 1927 issue of *Architectural Record*. Photographs ac-

CLIFF DWELLER APARTMENTS
96th Street and Riverside Drive, New York, New York, 1916

OPPOSITE
Mountain lions, kachina masks, and buffalo heads fill the frieze of the Cliff Dweller apartment house in New York City, an outstanding example of the Pueblo Deco style.

LEFT
The exterior decoration of the Cliff Dweller apartments includes Navajo directional motifs and kachina mask imagery.

RIGHT
Dating from 1916, the Cliff Dweller apartments are precocious. Few architects other than Mary Colter were working in the Pueblo Deco style at this early date. The architect, Herman Meader, focused attention on the building's penthouse with stepped pylons and terraced diamond patterns woven into the brickwork.

company Rose Henderson's article which describes the herringbone ceiling, the colors, and the patterns. She wrote that, "Like the typical Indian blanket, this decorative design is a primitive, desert-born thing, and in the proper setting (out of place in the ordinary modern interior) is as effective as a rattlesnake against yellow sand." (31) Other interiors were published during the twenties. Gerald Cassidy's home in Santa Fe was published, also in *Architectural Record*. His home contained actual beams and carved doors taken from the abandoned Mission church at Nambe Pueblo.

Another, later, apartment building, Gramercy House, is the only other dwelling in New York that was built in the Pueblo Deco style.

BIBLIOGRAPHY

Alexander, H. B. *The World's Rim: Great Mysteries of the North American Indians.* Lincoln: University of Nebraska Press, 1953.

Amsden, C. A. *Navajo Weaving: Its Technique and History.* Salt Lake City and Santa Barbara: Peregrine Smith, Inc., 1975.

Boas, F. *Primitive Art.* New York: Dover Publications, 1955.

Bossom, A. "Will Mexico Influence Our Architecture?" *Arts & Decoration*, March 1924, pp. 48–50.

Bunting, B. *Early Architecture in New Mexico.* Albuquerque: University of New Mexico Press, 1976.

———. *John Gaw Meem: Southwest Architect.* Albuquerque: University of New Mexico Press, 1984.

Chapman, A. "Sand Paintings of the American Desert." *Travel*, January 1921, pp. 15–17.

Cohen, J. *Cowtown Moderne: Art Deco Architecture of Fort Worth, Texas.* College Station Texas: Texas A & M University Press, 1988.

Colter, M. E. J. "Manual for Drivers and Guides Descriptive of The Indian Watchtower at Desert View and its Relation, Architecturally, to the Prehistoric Ruins of the Southwest." Arizona: Fred Harvey/Grand Canyon National Park, 1933.

Craig, L. and the Staff of Federal Architects Project. *The Federal Presence: Architecture, Politics, and Symbols in U.S. Government Buildings.* Cambridge: MIT Press, 1977.

Cushing, F. H. *My Adventures in Zuni.* Palo Alto, California: American West Publishing Company, 1905.

Davis, M. P. "Nomination Form—National Register of Historic Places Inventory: 1930 Federal Building, Albuquerque, New Mexico, 1980."

Dewitt, S. V. *Historic Albuquerque Today: An Overview Survey of Historic Buildings and Districts.* Albuquerque: Historic Landmarks Survey of Albuquerque, 1978.

———. "Nomination Form—National Register of Historic Places Inventory: Indian Hospital, Albuquerque, New Mexico, 1980."

Droege, J. A. *Passenger Terminals and Trains.* New York: McGraw-Hill, 1916.

Dunne, D. D. *American Indian Painting of the Southwest and Plains.* Albuquerque: University of New Mexico Press, 1968.

"El Navajo Hotel Brings Sand Paintings into the Pathway of Tourist Travel." *Albuquerque Journal*, May 27, 1923.

Engelbrecht, L. C. and J. M. F. *Henry C. Trost, Architect of the Southwest.* El Paso, Texas: El Paso Public Library Association, 1981.

Farb, P. *Man's Rise to Civilization As Shown By the Indians of North America From Primeval Times to the Coming of the Industrial State.* New York: E.P. Dutton & Co., Inc., 1968.

Fergusson, E. *Albuquerque.* Albuquerque: Merle Armitage Editions, 1947.

Fewkes, J. W. *Designs on Prehistoric Hopi Pottery.* Smithsonian Institution, Thirty Third Annual Report of the Bureau of American Enthology 1911–1912, Washington, D.C., 1919.

Fitting, J. E. *The Development of North American Architecture.* University Park: Penn State University Press, 1973.

Frankel, P. T. *New Dimensions: The Decorative Arts of Today in Words and Pictures.* New York: Payson, Payson & Clarke Ltd., 1928.

Frankenberger, R. "Les Mahoney: The Early Years." *Triglyph*, Winter, 1988–89, pp. 3–10.

Fred Harvey Archives. AmFac Corporation, Flagstaff, Arizona.

Gamarra, F. G. "Ancient Art Inspires New Decorative Vogue." *Arts & Decoration*, December 1923, pp. 38–39.

Gebhard, D. "Architecture and the Fred Harvey House." *New Mexico Architecture*, July-August 1962, pp. 12–17.

———. "Architecture and the Fred Harvey Houses: The Alvarado and La Fonda." *New Mexico Architecture*, January–February 1964, pp. 18–25.

———, and VonBreton, H. *LA in the Thirties, 1931–1941.* Salt Lake City: Peregrine Smith, 1975.

Gratton, V. L. *Mary Colter: Builder Upon the Red Earth.* Flagstaff, Arizona: Northland Press, 1980.

Henderson, R. "A Primitive Basis for Modern Architecture." *Architectural Record*, July–December 1923.

———. "The Spanish-Indian Tradition in Interior Decoration." *Architectural Record*, January–June 1927, pp. 195–199.

Hewett, E. L. "Recent Southwest Art," *Art & Archeology*, January 1920, pp. 30–48.

Hitchcock, H. R. and Wright, F. L. *In the Nature of Materials: The Buildings of Frank Lloyd Wright 1887–1941.* New York: Hawthorn Books, 1942.

Hoshour, H. S. "Historic Structure Report of the KiMo." Santa Fe: Historic Preservation Bureau, 1980.

Hunt, W. D. Jr. *Encyclopedia of American Architecture.* New York: McGraw Hill Book Co., 1980.

Iowa, J. "Plaza for Pyramid: The Anazazi Architectural Revolution." *Triglyph*, Fall 1984, pp. 29–32.

James, W. "Mission Pueblo Architecture in New Mexico." *Overland*, May 1919, pp. 382–388.

Knudsen, D. "Indian Basketry Art in the Alwahnee Hotel—Yosemite Valley." *The Architect and Engineer*, November 1928, pp. 51–56.

Kramer, J. J. *The Last of the Grand Hotels.* New York: Van Nostrand Reinhold Company, New York, 1984.

Langdon, P. *Orange Roofs, Golden Arches.* New York: Alfred A. Knopf, Inc., 1986.

Lavender, D. *The Southwest.* Albuquerque: University of New Mexico Press, 1980.

Luhrs Papers, Arizona Collection, University Library, Arizona State University.

Lynes, R. *The Tastemakers: The Shaping of American Popular Taste.* New York: Harper & Brothers, 1955.

Mason, O. T. *Aboriginal American Indian Basketry: Studies in a Textile Art Without Machinery.* Santa Barbara and Salt Lake City: Peregrine Smith, Inc., 1976.

Mather, C. "Nomination Form–National Register of Historic Places Inventory: Shaffer Hotel, Mountainair, New Mexico, 1980."

McArthur, W. Jr. "The Arizona Biltmore, The McArthur Brothers, and Frank Lloyd Wright." 35–46, *Triglyph*, Fall 1988.

McLuhan, T. C. *Dream Tracks: The Railroad and the American Indian, 1890–1930.* New York: Abrams, 1985.

John Gaw Meen Archives, University of New Mexico, Albuquerque, New Mexico.

Mooney, J. *The Ghost Dance Religion and the Sioux Outbreak of 1890.* Smithsonian Institution, 14th Annual Report of the Bureau of American Ethnology, Washington, D.C., 1892–93.

Nequatewa, E. *Truth of a Hopi: Stories Relating to the Origin, Myths and Clan Histories of the Hopi.* Museum of Northern Arizona Bulletin No. 8. Flagstaff: The Museum of Northern Arizona, 1936.

New York Terra Cotta Collection, Avery Library, Columbia University.

Onderdonk, F. S. *The Ferro-Concrete Style: Reinforced Concrete in Modern Architecture.* New York: Architectural Book Publishing Co., Inc., 1928.

Page, C. F. and Associates, Inc. *Amarillo Historic Building Survey and Preservation Program Recommendations.* Amarillo, Texas: City of Amarillo, 1981.

Paris, W. F. "The International Exposition of Modern Industrial and Decorative Art in Paris." *Architectural Record,* October 1925, pp. 365–387.

Price, C. M., "The Panama-California Exposition." *Architectural Record,* March 1915, p. 242.

Reps, J. W. *Town Planning in Frontier America.* Princeton: Princeton University Press, 1963.

Rittenberry Archives, Panhandle Plains Museum, Canyon, Texas.

Robinson, C. and Bletter, R. H. *Skyscraper Style: Art Deco New York.* New York: Oxford University Press, 1975.

Rollins, P. A. *The Cowboy: An Unconventional History of Civilization On the Old Time Cattle Range.* Albuquerque: University of New Mexico Press, 1979.

Sanford, T. E. *The Architecture of the Southwest.* New York: W.W. Norton & Co., 1950.

Sargent, S. *The Ahwahnee: Yosemite's Classic Hotel.* Yosemite, California: Flying Spur Press, 1984.

Schmidt, R. *Fort Worth & Tarrant County, A Historic Guide.* Fort Worth: Texas Christian University Press, 1984.

Sexton, R. W., *The Logic of Modern Architecture.* New York Architectural Book Publishing, 1929.

Sheppard, C. D. *Creator of the Santa Fe Style: Isaac Hamilton Rapp.* Albuquerque: University of New Mexico Press, 1988.

Short, C. W. and Stanley-Brown, R. *Public Buildings: A Survey of Architecture of Projects Constructed by Federal and Other Governmental Bodies Between the Years 1933 and 1939.* Washington, D.C.: U.S. Government Printing Office, 1939.

Simms, A.F. "Pueblo—A Native American Architecture." *House & Garden,* April 1922, pp. 52–84.

Solon, L. V. "Modernism in Architecture," *Architectural Record,* September 1926, pp. 193–201.

Tanner, C. L. *Southwest Indian Craft Arts.* Tucson: University of Arizona Press, 1968.

"Terra Cotta Towers." *Atlantic Terra Cotta,* January 1928, pp. 1–22.

Thomas, D. H. *The Southwestern Indian Detours: The Story of the Fred Harvey/Santa Fe Railway Experiment in "Detourism."* Phoenix, Arizona: Hunter Publishing Co., 1978.

Trent, E. S. *The Architecture of the Southwest, Indian, Spanish, American.* New York: W. W. Norton & Co., Inc., 1950.

"Two Thousand Tons of Terra Cotta: New York Central Building." *Atlantic Terra Cotta,* March 1929, pp. 1–4.

Underhill, R. M. *Redman's America.* Chicago: University of Chicago Press, 1953.

Walker, W. and Wyckoff, L. L. *Hopis, Tewas and the American Road.* Middletown, Connecticut: Wesleyan University Press, 1983.

Ward, F. E. *The Cowboy at Work.* New York: Hastings House, 1958.

Whiffen, M. *American Architecture Since 1780.* Cambridge: MIT Press, 1967.

———and Breeze, C. *Pueblo Deco: The Art Deco Architecture of the Southwest.* Albuquerque: University of New Mexico Press, 1983.

Wilson, C. "Nomination Form—National Register of Historic Places Inventory: Mountainair Municipal Auditorium, 1986."

Withey, H. F. and Withey, E. R. *Biographical Dictionary of American Architects (Deceased).* Los Angeles: New Age Publishing Co., 1956.

Wright, B. *Hopi Kachinas: The Complete Guide to Collecting Kachina Dolls.* Flagstaff, Arizona: Northland Press, 1977.

INTERVIEWS

Carlander, Mary. Interview with author and Marcus Whiffen, April 19, 1981, Amarillo, Texas.

Gaut, J. Interview with author, June 5, 1989, Amarillo, Texas.

Lee, Antoinette. Interview with author, May 12, 1989, via telephone.

McArthur, Warren. Interview with author, April 17, 1988, Clovis, New Mexico.

Merrell, Billy. Interview with author, February 24, 1981, Clovis, New Mexico.

Rittenberry, James. Interview with author, June 2, 1989, via telephone.

Thomas, Bernice. Interview with author, February 23, 1989, via telephone.

NOTES

ONE

1　L. Craig and the Staff of Federal Architects Project. *The Federal Presence: Architecture, Politics, and Symbols in U. S. Government Buildings.* Cambridge: MIT Press, 1977, p. 278.

2　M. E. J. Colter. "Manual for Drivers and Guides Descriptive of the Indian Watchtower at Desert View and its Relation, Architecturally, to the Prehistoric Ruins of the Southwest." Arizona: Fred Harvey/Grand Canyon National Park, 1933, p. 11.

3　P.A. Rollins. *The Cowboy: An Unconventional History of Civilization on the Old Time Cattle Range.* Albuquerque: University of New Mexico Press, 1979, p. 2.

4　J. A. Droege. *Passenger Terminals and Trains.* New York: McGraw-Hill, 1916, p. 12.

5　O. Wister. "A Preface by Owen Wister." New York: Architectural Book Publishing Co., 1923, p. 1.

6　Advertisement for Atchison Topeka & Santa Fe Railroad, c.1925.

7　D. H. Thomas. *The Southwestern Indian Detours: The Story of Fred Harvey/Santa Fe Railway Experiment in "Detourism."* Phoenix, Arizona: Hunter Publishing Co., 1978, p. 65.

8　J. G. Meem. Notes from conversation with client. John Gaw Meem Collection, University of New Mexico Library, Special Collections, Albuquerque, New Mexico, 1935.

9　A. Chapman. "Indian Fair," *Art and Archeology.* 1924, p. 224.

TWO

10　R. Henderson. "The Spanish-Indian Tradition in Interior Decoration." *Architectural Record.* January-June 1927, pp. 196–197.

11　"Eyes of State Turn to Clovis Where its Tallest Rears Aloft." *Clovis Evening News,* October 19, 1931, section 2, p. 1.

12　C. Mather. "Nomination Form—National Register of Historic Places Inventory: Shaffer Hotel, Mountainair, New Mexico, 1980."

13　V. L. Gratton. *Mary Colter: Builder Upon Red Earth.* Flagstaff: Northland Press, 1980, p. 52.

14　"The Arizona Biltmore." *Architectural Record,* November 1929.

15　R. W. Sexton. *The Logic of Modern Architecture.* New York: Architectural Book Publishing Co., 1929, p. 48.

16　D. Knudsen. "Indian Basketry Art in the Ahwahnee Hotel—Yosemite Valley." *The Architect and Engineer,* November 1928, p. 52.

17　S. Sargent. *The Ahwahnee: Yosemite's Classic Hotel.* Yosemite, California: Flying Spur Press, 1984, p. 19.

FOUR

18　C. W. Short and R. Stanley-Brown. *Public Buildings: A Survey of Architecture of Projects Constructed by Federal and Other Governmental Bodies Between the Years 1933 and 1939.* Washington, D. C.: U. S. Government Printing Office, 1939, p. VI.

19　ibid. p. VIII.

20　ibid. p. XII.

21　P. T. Frankel. *New Dimensions: The Decorative Arts of Today in Words and Pictures.* New York: Payson & Clarke Ltd., 1928, p. 29.

22　Undated, untitled newspaper article in scrapbook at Panhandle Plains Museum, Canyon, Texas.

23　M. Whiffen and C. Breeze. *Pueblo Deco: The Art Deco Architecture of the Southwest.* Albuquerque: University of New Mexico Press, 1983, p. 56.

24　ibid. p. 24.

FIVE

25　"Small Buildings of Atlantic Terra Cotta." *Atlantic Terra Cotta,* February 1928, p. 1.

26　ibid. Preface.

27　"Buildings for S. H. Kress and Company New York City." *Architectural Forum,* February 1936, p. 88.

28　Letter from H. Jerome Toy of H. Jerome Toy and Company, Promoters and Financial Agents to George Luhrs, dated October 28, 1928. Luhrs Papers, Arizona Collection, University Library, Arizona State University.

29　Frankel. p. 114.

SIX

30　"Our Lady of Precious Blood Church." *Atlantic Terra Cotta,* April 1932, p. 9.

SEVEN

31　Henderson. p. 197.

CREDITS

P.34　Drawing courtesy Zimmerman Library Archives, University of New Mexico.

P.90　Rendering courtesy Amarillo Public Library.

P.92　Drawing courtesy J. Gaut, Amarillo, Texas.

P.98　Top: Drawing copyright © 1942 Frank Lloyd Wright Foundation, courtesy Taliesin.
　　　Bottom: Drawing copyright © 1985 Frank Lloyd Wright Foundation, courtesy Taliesin.

P.99　Drawing copyright © 1959 Frank Lloyd Wright Foundation, courtesy Taliesin.